25.95 BF

D0219475

UNDERSTANDING THE SELF–EGO RELATIONSHIP IN CLINICAL PRACTICE: TOWARDS INDIVIDUATION

CCU Library
8787 W. Alameda Ave.
Lakewood, CO 80226

The Society of Analytical Psychology Monograph Series
Hazel Robinson (Series Editor)
Published and distributed by Karnac Books

Other titles in the SAP Monograph Series

Understanding Narcissism in Clinical Practice
  Hazel Robinson & Victoria Graham Fuller

Understanding Perversion in Clinical Practice:
Structure and Strategy in the Psyche
  Fiona Ross

Orders
Tel: +44 (0)20 8969 4454; Fax: +44 (0)20 8969 5585
Email: shop@karnacbooks.com

UNDERSTANDING THE SELF–EGO RELATIONSHIP IN CLINICAL PRACTICE: TOWARDS INDIVIDUATION

Margaret Clark

KARNAC

LONDON   NEW YORK

First published in 2006 by
H. Karnac (Books) Ltd.
6 Pembroke Buildings, London NW10 6RE

Copyright © 2006 Margaret Clark

The right of Margaret Clark to be identified as the author of
this work has been asserted in accordance with §§ 77 and 78
of the Copyright Design and Patents Act 1988.

All rights reserved. No part of this publication may be repro-
duced, stored in a retrieval system, or transmitted, in any
form or by any means, electronic, mechanical, photocopying,
recording, or otherwise, without the prior written permission
of the publisher.

British Library Cataloguing in Publication Data

A C.I.P. for this book is available from the British Library

ISBN: 1 85575 388 X

Edited, designed and produced by The Studio Publishing
Services Ltd
www.publishingservicesuk.co.uk
e-mail: studio@publishingservicesuk.co.uk

Printed in Great Britain by Hobbs the Printers Ltd, Totton, Hampshire

www.karnacbooks.com

Contents

Contents

About the Author

Margaret Clark trained as a psychodynamic counsellor and a psychoanalytic psychotherapist at **wpf** counselling/psychotherapy before she trained as a Jungian analyst at the Society of Analytical Psychology in London. She is now a Training Analyst and Supervisor for the British Association of Psychotherapists and a Training Analyst of the SAP. She works in private practice in London.

CCU Library
CCU Library Ave.
Lakewood, CO 80226
Lakewood, CO 80226

Preface to the Series

This series of clinical practice monographs is being produced primarily for the benefit of trainees on psychotherapy and psychodynamic counselling courses. The authors are Jungian analysts who have trained at the Society of Analytical Psychology, with extensive experience of teaching both theory and practice.

The rationale for this series is in part to do with the expensive and time-consuming task of accessing all the pertinent books and papers for any one clinical subject. These single-issue monographs have been kept relatively brief and cannot claim to be comprehensive, but we hope that each volume brings together some of the major theorists and their ideas in a comprehensible way, including references to significant and interesting texts.

Much of the literature provided for students of psychotherapy has been generated from four or five-times weekly analytic work, which can be confusing for students whose psychodynamic courses may be structured on the basis of less frequent sessions. The authors of these monographs have aimed to hold this difference in mind. A decision was taken to maintain the terms 'therapist' and 'patient' throughout, although the clinical work referred to ranges from once weekly to five-times weekly. We have borrowed gratefully from the work of our supervisees in many settings, and we are above all indebted to our patients. Where a patient's material is recognizable, their permission to publish has been given. In other cases, we have amalgamated and disguised clinical material to preserve anonymity.

When a training is 'eclectic', that is, offering several different psychodynamic perspectives, a particular difficulty can arise with integration – or rather *non*-integration of psychoanalytic and Jungian analytic ideas. The teaching on such trainings is often presented in blocks: a term devoted to 'Freud', another to 'Jung', and so on. It is frequently the students who are left with the job of trying to see where these do and do not fit together, and this can be a daunting, even depressing, experience. SAP analysts are in a better position than most to offer some help here, because its members have been working on this integration since the organization was founded in 1946. Although retaining a strong relationship with 'Zurich' or 'Classical' Jungian scholarship, SAP members have evolved equally strong links with psychoanalysis. Recent years have brought a number of joint conferences to supplement the many 'cross-party' alliances.

Any patient, but particularly a trainee, will naturally tend to adopt the language of his or her therapist when talking about their work. Those readers who are unfamiliar with Jungian terms may wish to consult the *Critical Dictionary of Jungian Analysis* (Samuels, Shorter & Plaut, 1986), while those unfamiliar with psychoanalytic terms may turn to *The Language of Psychoanalysis* (Laplanche & Pontalis, 1988). But all patients are united by their human suffering far more than they are divided by language. Just as people from non-western cultures have to make what they can of their western-trained psychotherapists, so each patient–therapist pair eventually evolves a unique way of understanding their joint experiences in the consulting-room. It is our view that each stream of psychotherapy has strengths and weaknesses, and the wise trainee will take the best bits from each. We hope that this series may help a little with the psychodynamic 'Tower of Babel'.

We want to thank Karnac for their patience and help in bringing the series to publication. Our intention is to gradually add further volumes on some of the principal clinical issues. I therefore want to end by thanking my colleagues within the SAP for their work so far – and for their work to come.

Hazel Robinson
Series Editor

Introduction

'How does one come to terms in
practice with the unconscious?'
(Jung, 1957, p. 67)

The clinical value of thinking about the relations between the ego and the self is that it makes us take the self seriously. It shifts our focus. It brings into all our work with the patient a constant awareness of the self. Some schools of psychotherapy focus totally on the development of the ego; and psychodynamic and psychoanalytic psychotherapy may need, with some patients, at some stages of the work, to focus on their ego capacities and try to help them function more adequately and more comfortably in their external world. This can be a necessary preliminary to the more fundamental work of facilitating a dialogue between the newly strengthened ego and the threatening, overflowing unconscious psyche. But even in work that remains with this more limited aim, it is based on the therapist mediating a negotiation between the patient's ego and their self.

For, primarily, this mode of psychotherapy is not aiming to supply ego-solutions. It struggles with the question: 'How does one come to terms in practice with the unconscious?' (Jung, 1957, p. 67). It tries to facilitate deep and lasting psychic change based on a new relation between the patient's ego and self. This change is likely, of itself, to produce its own ego-solutions; but they will then be more soundly based, growing out of the patient's own new internal structures, rather than having been learned and applied externally. This is the most stark dividing line between those who work psychoanalytically and psychodynamically, and those who work cognitively and behaviourally.

Cognitive and behavioural work can benefit some patients enormously; and many suffering people are not suited to psychoanalytic and psychodynamic psychotherapy, usually because their ego is not strong enough to sustain an increased awareness of their self. But if it is possible to facilitate a dialogue between the ego and the self, rather than building a stronger wall to protect the ego from the self, then we are engaging in work with long-term potential not only for healing but also for what Jung calls individuation – a process where more of a person's unconscious psyche enters their conscious awareness – where more of their self is realized. One patient spoke of his reason for coming into therapy: 'I want to understand more,' he said. A few sessions later he added: 'If I understand more, I shall be in a better position to choose.' This precisely expresses the strengthening of the ego (a greater capacity to choose) as a direct result of his understanding more of his unconscious psyche. Current studies in neuroscience also tell us that long-term, intensive psychoanalytic psychotherapy changes a patient's brain structure: the changes are lasting, inscribed not only in the psyche but also in the body (Tresan, 1996, p. 416; Beebe & Lachman, 2002, p. 228).

An overview of the book

The purpose of the book, therefore, is to discuss, and to illustrate with clinical vignettes, the different ways in which a person's ego and self can relate to each other. A developmental model is used. Differences between theorists are considered. In the later chapters, the emphasis is on Jung's (and post-Jungian) theory, since it is here that we find the strongest theoretical basis for viewing a potential dialogue between self and ego as useful for a person's psychic development.

Chapter One examines the development of models of the unconscious psyche, and Chapter Two goes on to consider the complexities of defining the concepts of ego and self.

Chapter Three looks at different ways of thinking about the contents of the unconscious psyche, in particular the difference it can make to our clinical practice whether we think of 'internal objects' or of 'sub-personalities'.

Chapter Four considers how different theoreticians view the development of the ego in infancy, how this newly emerging ego relates to the infant self, and what this means in our clinical work with adults. Chapter Five thinks about those adult patients who still need to complete these childhood tasks, and for whom the clinical work is primarily to strengthen the developing ego. Various ways in which the ego is not able to integrate messages from the self are illustrated with clinical vignettes.

Chapter Six considers how the therapist can use an awareness of their own self–ego relationship.

Chapters Seven and Eight consider the later stages of the process of individuation. Chapter Seven focuses primarily on intrapsychic development – on therapy with people whose ego is strong enough to engage constructively with their unconscious psyche, and for whom a 'dialogue' between ego and self is beneficial. The power and purpose of the newly found symbol is seen as central to this process. Chapter Eight focuses more on individuation through relationships – through dialogue with other people. It considers how withdrawing projections from other people leads simultaneously to a greater knowledge both of one's own self and of the other person: relationship with a genuinely 'other' person becomes possible. Our ethical responsibility both to our own selves and also to others, to society, is considered.

All the clinical material is an amalgam of experiences with different people; none represents an actual person.

CHAPTER ONE

THE UNCONSCIOUS PSYCHE

'I may allow myself only one criterion for
the result of my labours: Does it work?'
(Jung, 1929a, p. 43)

Theoreticians of different schools are usually trying to describe the same observed phenomena, but our theoretical stance subtly affects what we observe, as well as how we explain it, often without our being aware of it. This unconscious theoretical bias can even affect what we consider pathological, as well as affecting clinical decisions about management or technique.

Not all psychological theorists even agree that there is an unconscious psyche at all. Jung wrote: 'I regard the psyche as *real*' (Jung, 1952a, p. 464; original italics), and all depth psychologists, all who practise psychoanalytic or psychodynamic psychotherapy, would agree. But even for these clinicians and theorists, it can be hard to give full-blooded credence to the idea that our patients' fantastical stories are as 'real' as external reality. They are equally real (in making psychic impact) because any reality we can know is processed in the same way: our brain receives sensations from the external world or stimuli from our internal world of fantasy, images and dreams; and then our brain interprets the resultant patterns and gives them meaning. We may think it is our mind/psyche which gives them meaning, rather than our brain. Our body is the interface between internal and external reality; both worlds are equally objective to what we call our ego, and our apprehension of both is mediated by the same instrument. The implications of this point of view can still surprise and shock us: for instance, that to consider our dreams in the morning, or to say our prayers, may be as important and meaningful as greeting our family. And clinically it can prepare the therapist to consider that there may be a connection between a patient's speaking of the weight of her shopping bags just before relating a dream of killing her husband: the fact that she is speaking consecutively of both these 'objective' experiences suggests that she as a subject has made a connection (which can then be explored together) between her external and internal reality.

Establishing the existence of the unconscious psyche

Freud and Jung both thought of themselves as continuing the work of other physicians who were, at the end of the nineteenth century, exploring manifestations of unconscious activity – Janet, Forel, Flournoy, Prince, Bleuler. For both, their main concern was that the very existence of the unconscious psyche should be acknowledged. Freud laid his reputation on the line with the publication of 'The interpretation of dreams' (1900a). He delayed publishing this for four years, because he imagined a furore of disagreement over his theory that the psychic mechanism of repression created unconscious material that could then disturb consciousness. (In fact, his book was largely ignored: only 351 copies were sold in the first six years after publication.) Freud and Jung were both concerned that they might be considered academically or scientifically unsound, because of their belief in the existence of the unconscious psyche.

In 1900, when Jung took up his post at the Burghölzli mental hospital, most theoretical psychologists and physicians thought 'there was no psyche outside the ego', though poets and philosophers had long known of unconscious motivations (Jung, 1944, p. 480). At the Burghölzli, he was alone in asking about his psychotic patients,

> why this patient had one kind of fantasy, another an altogether different one; or what it signified when, for instance, a patient had the fantasy of being persecuted by the Jesuits, or when another imagined that the Jews wanted to poison him, or a third was convinced that the police were after him. Such questions seemed altogether uninteresting to doctors of those days. (Jung, 1962, p. 149)

Indeed, such questions still seem uninteresting to many doctors of these days.

But Jung wrote that at that time he 'realized that paranoid ideas and hallucinations contain a germ of meaning'. He listened, sometimes over many years, to patients considered beyond hope or help. He assumed that their fantastical stories conveyed a psychic reality. One young woman, who had been sexually abused by her brother, had retreated from this unbearable reality into another reality, the fantasy of living on the moon. In the hospital she heard voices, refused food, and was mute. After many weeks, she told Jung about her life on the moon, and her heroic mission there to kill the demon-vampire and rescue the women in his thrall. Jung understood her fantasy as elevating her to royal status (since incest is historically the prerogative of royalties and divinities) and as giving her life sublime meaning and importance, in compensation for her humiliation at the hands of her abuser. His under-standing enabled her, with deep reluctance and several retreats into insanity, to return to a life on earth, and to leave the hospital (Jung, 1962, pp. 148–152).

Apart from his work with his patients at the Burghölzli, Jung's exploration into unconscious activity consisted at this time of his word association tests (1904). In these tests, the subject was asked to respond immediately to each word on a list with an associated word; the time before he responded to each word was noted, and Jung found that a longer delay corresponded with something of emotional significance (to the subject) in the trigger word. Scientifically it was proven: something was disturbing the conscious response to the word given – therefore, there was something else in the psyche apart from conscious-ness. Jung was triumphant that he had provided scientific evidence (contrasted, as he saw it, with the anecdotal evidence in Freud's book) for Freud's hypothesis that there was an unconscious aspect to the psyche – though later he also remembered that he had been reluctant to associate himself with someone (Freud) who was *persona non grata* in academic circles (Jung, 1962, p. 170).

Yet, as late as 1947, we find Jung arguing, extensively and in detail, for the very existence of an unconscious aspect of the psyche, as a matter 'of absolutely revolution-ary significance in that it could radically alter our view of the world' (Jung, 1947, p. 178). And in 1962 he still has to acknowledge that 'the assimilation of the fundamental insight that psychic life has two poles still remains a task for the future' (Jung, 1962, p. 193).

This task is not yet completed. Today, cognitive behavi-oural therapists and authors of self-help books routinely treat our unconscious psyche like a repressive parent treats

4

a naughty child: they ignore it, tell it to keep quiet, send it to its room. Biological determinists among psychiatrists show no greater respect for it: for them chemical imbalances cause mental illness; drugs are the only appropriate treatment. Among many general practitioners and medical specialists there is little awareness of a psychic component to a somatic illness. The power of our unconscious psyche to affect our bodies, our adaptation to external reality, our personal relationships, our capacity to learn and to work and to live as good citizens in our community: this is not commonly recognized. It is a force not reckoned with in the organization of our health care, or of our educational, social, legal, or political systems. Even many of our mainstream religious systems don't know how to handle it, though there are strong trends within them, as well as in some more marginal traditions, which pay it great attention.

The various theoretical approaches discussed in Chapter Two are all those of depth psychologists who do acknowledge the existence and the power of the unconscious psyche. We need concepts as essential tools so that we can think, but the sole purpose of a model, in our clinical work, is to help us understand what is happening in the session – in our own mind, in the mind of the patient, and in the interaction between the two. The criterion is: does it work? That is, does it fit with what we are experiencing? Does interpreting according to this model help the patient? Do we feel comfortable with it?

Models of the unconscious psyche

Freud referred to the 'System Unconscious'; the 'subconscious' of popular parlance is not a term used in psychoanalytic writings. This 'System Unconscious', which Freud later renamed as the 'id', is the home of our instincts. Also unconscious are preconscious experiences (which could easily be available again to the ego) and repressed experiences (which the ego cannot tolerate knowing); these are all experiences that have been conscious. These are akin to what Jung calls the personal unconscious, which he distinguishes from the collective unconscious.

Jung sometimes refers to the unconscious psyche as 'the objective psyche' because it is experienced by the conscious ego, the 'I', the thinking subject, as distinct, as an object of its thought and not part of its own subjectivity. It is autonomous. Freud similarly understood that contents of the unconscious act independently of the ego, but he attributed purpose to the id only in its blind seeking for instinctual gratification. Otherwise, purpose comes from the ego, which uses the unconscious psyche as a repository for experiences it wants out of its mind.

Jung (1928a, p. 123) is perhaps overstating his claim for originality when he writes that '[t]his idea of the independence of the unconscious, which distinguishes my ideas so radically from those of Freud, came to me as far back as 1902' (from his word-association experiments). After his break with Freud in 1912, this idea was reinforced by his experience of holding conversations with Philemon and other fantasy figures. He discovered that the unconscious psyche has its own independent and purposeful life:

Philemon represented a force which was not myself. . . . He said . . . 'If you should see people in a room, you would not think that you had made those people, or that you were responsible for them.' It was he who taught me psychic objectivity, the reality of the psyche. (Jung, 1962, pp. 207f.)

Let us not forget, however, that, many centuries before, Saint Augustine had said, 'Thank God I am not responsible for my dreams' (cf. Jung 1916, p. 245) – an earlier acknowledgement, with relief, of the autonomy of the unconscious psyche, and a position Freud would have agreed with.

Central to Jung's understanding of the psyche is his concept of the collective unconscious. He considered this as '*inherited*' (Jung, 1941, p. 155; original italics), autonomous, containing our common psychic inheritance and, not being limited by what we have ourselves put into it, theoretically limitless. None of us owns it; we all participate in it. He writes:

Life has always seemed to me like a plant that lives on its rhizome. Its true life is invisible, hidden in the rhizome. The part that appears above ground lasts only a single summer. Then it withers away – an ephemeral apparition. When we think of the unending growth and decay of life and civilizations, we cannot escape the impression of absolute nullity. Yet I have never lost a sense of something that lives and endures underneath the eternal flux. What we see is the blossom, which passes. The rhizome remains. (Jung, 1962, p. 18)

Freud also writes (1915e, p. 190) of the unconscious psyche as 'alive and capable of development'. His more usual emphasis, however, is on our 'inherited endowment, a phylogenetic heritage' (1918b, p. 97), primarily inherited memories of our ancestors' experiences, and he was, of course, particularly interested in the sexual elements.

Jung often uses language we usually associate with God to think about the collective unconscious. This analogy is not confined to Jung and Jungian theorists. Bomford, an Anglican priest, develops, through a study of the logic of Matte Blanco in relation to Freudian theories, the parallels between the way we understand God and the way we understand the unconscious psyche (Bomford, 1999). Both seem infinite and eternal, that is, they cannot be defined in ego-based concepts of space and time. Yet, since the conscious psyche is all we know, we have to define the un-conscious psyche in apposition to ego-based consciousness. To avoid the negative associations that he thought the prefix 'un' carries, Jung suggested other terminology: the 'transconscious' psyche, the 'non-conscious' psyche and the 'extra-conscious' psyche. Awareness of these alternatives can help to keep our minds limber, and prevent us from ossifying 'the unconscious' into a reified, static object.

Freud is more cautious, Jung more enthusiastic, in approaching the unconscious psyche. Jung revels in its potential richness and relies on its sustaining power, as well as warning of its capacity to overwhelm the ego. Klein focuses mainly on its destructiveness: she writes more about the infant's phantasies of oral sadism than about his phantasies of love; for example, she writes that love, potentially present from birth, is 'disturbed at its roots by destructive impulses', and that it develops 'in connection with aggressive impulses and in spite of them' (Klein, 1937, pp. 306, 308). Which emphasis we prefer will depend largely on our own temperament and experiences.

All theory is only relatively true

No theory about the psyche is absolutely 'true'. All are limited by the ways in which the psyche itself perceives unconscious contents in consciousness. All are hypotheses; and all are conditioned by the personality of the theorist and by their particular historical, cultural, and gendered perspective. For instance, we note that Freud was the eldest and favourite son of his mother; and that he analysed his own youngest daughter, Anna: and we note the emphasis in his theory on the Oedipus complex. We think these facts may be connected. Winnicott, when asked about his mother, replied merely, 'I had one'; and we note in contrast (perhaps in compensation) the emphasis in his theory on the importance of the mother–infant relationship. Jung wrote in 1962 that both his mother and he himself had a number one and a number two personality. The emphasis here is on dissociation rather than on dialogue, and we can think that his model of ego and self evolved from this early experience of 'disunion' with himself. As a child, and knowing he was only a schoolboy from a poor home, he had compensatory fantasies of grandeur and omnipotence: he had an inviolable secret: he had made and hidden in the attic the little manikin he came to associate with God (Jung, 1962, pp. 36, 42f., 109). Moreover, his greater reliance on an internal dialogue rather than on a dialogue with another person may be connected to the fact that his mother was from time to time in hospital and Jung in the care of a maid. We can see here part of the attraction and the danger in his theories of an encompassing self.

CHAPTER TWO

EGO AND SELF: DEFINING AND DIFFERENTIATING

'The individual investigator must at least try to
give his concepts some fixity and precision'
(Jung, 1921, p. 409)

This chapter presents some of the complications around
the various uses of the terms 'ego' and 'self', and addresses
the question: why does it matter?

The ego

There is a widespread consensus of opinion among theoreticians of varying schools to hypothesize a psychic
'organ', like a physical organ, and to call it 'the ego'. The
definition in *A Critical Dictionary of Jungian Analysis*
(Samuels, Shorter, & Plaut, 1986) would sit equally comfortably in Rycroft's *A Critical Dictionary of Psychoanalysis*
(1968), or in Hinshelwood's *A Dictionary of Kleinian
Thought* (1989). It would suit Fairbairn and Winnicott, as
well as most contemporary theorists. It reads: 'the ego is
concerned with such matters as personal identity, mainte-
nance of the personality, continuity over time, mediation
between conscious and unconscious realms, cognition and
reality testing' (Samuels, Shorter, & Plaut, 1986, p. 50).

It is only the next part of this sentence that distinguishes a Jungian view from that of all other theorists; it

reads: 'it [the ego] also has to be seen as responsive to the demands of something superior. This is the self, the ordering principle of the entire personality.' This part of the definition is to do with the place of the ego in the hierarchy of the psyche. For Jung in 1907, when he was 32 (Jung, 1907, p. 40), and for all other theorists, the ego is the king of the castle. Jung, however, came to consider the ego as an usurper, and the self as the rightful king.

There is a consensus that the ego is related to a person's experience of his or her body. But even this is not totally straightforward. Most people are referring here only to the limited field of our conscious experience of our bodily sensations. For instance, we are aware of our physical shape and of our skin as defining our boundary, of the extent of our reach with our arms, of our weight as we sit or move. We are aware of our bodies changing as we age. Some bodily functions we are conscious of and can in part control – walking, grasping, excreting (urine, faeces, spittle, tears).

In parallel with the way we consciously experience our body, we have an ego-based relationship to external and internal reality. In psychic health, we are aware of the limitations imposed on us by time and space as to what is physically and psychically possible. We can judge, more or less, what we can realistically reach out for, materially and emotionally, and what we can realistically and safely get rid of from our material possessions (left-over food, outgrown clothes) as well as from our emotions. People who think they can fly, for instance, or destroy the whole world with a sneeze, do not have an ego based in a realistic assessment of their bodily functions. And people who cannot get rid of material baggage (a hoard, whether of newspaper, yoghurt cartons, furniture, or money) are likely to have problems with getting rid of both their physical and their emotional waste.

Bodily functions over which we can have some control (such as breathing or our heartbeat) but which are largely involuntary and usually not part of our conscious awareness of our selves, relate partly to our unconscious psyche and partly to our ego (which Jung, like Freud, sometimes thinks of as being itself partly unconscious). As a bridge between our conscious and unconscious psyche, these functions are often the locus for psychosomatic symptoms, as some unconscious material strives to become conscious through a bodily manifestation.

Jung went further and considered the psychic representation of those bodily functions of which we are not aware and which we cannot control, such as the flow of our blood, the growth and decay of our cells, the processing of food by chemicals in our gut, kidney and liver, the working of our brain. He considers that these functions are represented in our unconscious psyche by the part of it he calls 'the collective unconscious' (Jung, 1941, pp. 172f.; see Chapter One).

The functions of the ego are viewed similarly by all major theorists, except for Lacan. He alone sees the ego quite differently, as an agent whose purpose is to misread the truth that comes to it from internal or external sources; for him, it is essentially narcissistic and distorting (Benvenuto & Kennedy, 1986, p. 60). By others it is seen as the organ of agency in negotiation with both external and internal reality.

There is more widespread dissent as to whether there is more to consciousness than the ego; there is controversy as to whether the ego exists at birth or not, and as to whether the ego develops out of the id, or out of the primary self, or whether the ego is primary and the self (meaning here a conscious sense of self) develops subsequent and consequent to the development of the ego.

Approaches to the self as a clinical concept

There is a widespread theoretical consensus that a person has a psychic experience that is to be called an experience of a self. The self is thus a name for another hypothetical psychic object. There is no consensus as to whether the self, like the ego, is a psychic organ of agency, or whether it is a more passive entity. There is greater complexity, and less consistency, in the use of the term 'the self' than there is with 'the ego'. This occurs both between different theorists and, often, within the work of any one; this complexity and lack of consistency is particularly apparent in Jung, where also the concept is of prime importance. There is a useful discussion by Redfearn of what he calls 'the present muddle' in the use of this terminology (Redfearn, 1985, pp. 1–18).

Hinshelwood writes that Klein 'often used "ego" interchangeably with "self"' (Hinshelwood, 1989, p. 284).

Kohut means something like 'a sense of personal identity' by his 'self'. But he also includes much of what others attribute to the ego, including agency and a sense of purposefulness (which he has in common with Jung). For him, the self is the 'core of the personality' (Kohut, 1984, pp. 4–7).

Winnicott writes of 'the maturational process', which 'refers to the evolution of the ego and of the self' (Winnicott, 1963, p. 85). This 'self' is related to the 'True

Self', which is a 'spontaneous' part of a person, and which, if it is not allowed to exist, is protected by the development of a compliant 'False Self' (Winnicott, 1960a, p. 145). Kalsched refers to these concepts of Winnicott when he writes of 'the personal spirit' and its archetypal defences (Kalsched, 1996, p. 3).

Stern, from a developmental perspective, writes of four senses of self and of how they develop in an infant and young child (Stern, 1985).

Fonagy and colleagues relate attachment theory to the child's development of a capacity for reflective function-ing and a sense of self; they consider how the self is also an agent in the child's development (Fonagy, Gergely, Jurist, & Target, 2002, p. 24).

Rycroft defines the self in psychoanalytic theory thus: 'the self refers to the subject as he experiences himself while the ego refers to his personality as a structure about which impersonal generalizations can be made' (Rycroft, 1968, p. 149).This version of the psychoanalytic self is defined specifically as excluding any unconscious parts of the psyche. It reflects common, non-technical usage.

Milrod sums up the varying uses of the term in later psychoanalytic literature: the term may refer to the individual or person, to his ego as a psychic structure, to a psychic representation of the individual, to a super-ordinate fourth psychic structure alongside the id, ego and super-ego, or to a fantasy. His own view is that the psychic representation of the self comes to be a substructure within the ego (Milrod, 2002, pp. 8f.).

Jung, on the other hand, uses the term 'the self' specifi-cally to include the unconscious psyche, and for him it is specifically not contained within the ego. For him, the self stands over against the ego, or, at different stages of psychic development, contains it. It is a major theoretical difference between psychoanalysis and analytical psychology, and has clinical repercussions. Jung developed his concept slowly and often not consistently, as part of his struggle to define, and to have recognized, the collective unconscious. He first uses the term 'the self' in 1916, but there is no separate entry for 'self' in the 'Definitions' at the end of *Psychological Types* in 1921. Forty years later, he added it, for the *Collected Works* of 1960. Here he defines it as 'the unity of the personality as a whole'; it is 'psychic totality, consisting of both conscious and unconscious contents', and therefore is 'only a working hypothesis', since what is unconscious cannot be known (Jung, 1921, pp. 460f.). At other times, or on the way to this definition, he also uses the term to mean our unconscious psyche, or all of our conscious and unconscious psyche which is not ego. With any of these meanings, it is possible to think of a dialogue between the ego and the self, and that the self is 'king'.

Structures of the self: different hypotheses – id, unconscious phantasy, archetype

Freud and Klein both consider that the ego is the main organized part of the psyche. Both write also about the structure of the super-ego, and struggle with whether the id also has any innate structure, or capacity to encourage the structuring of our experiences, aside from our physical, instinctual responses. They do not, of course, think in this context of a 'self'.

Freud thought that the id has no organization, and no purpose beyond satisfying instinctual needs and seeking pleasure. Yet, from 1916–1917 through to the year of his death in 1939, he writes also of the 'memory-traces in the archaic heritage' that dispose us to react in a particular manner to particular stimuli; these memory-traces probably include subject matter as well as dispositions, and can be remembered as an alternative to remembering personal experience when the personal memory fails (Freud 1916–1917, p. 199; 1939a, pp. 98ff.; cf. also 1918b, p. 97).

Klein saw unconscious phantasy as present from birth to structure instinctual impulses in mental representations (the formation of internal objects). (The spelling 'phantasy' is a useful way of distinguishing unconscious phantasy from fantasies, which are conscious.) Klein considers that the baby's own impulses, emotions, and phantasies are 'innate'; they meet with external reality (through projection). The modified re-introjected experience that forms the nucleus of an internal object is an amalgam of this meeting of a pre-existing internal phantasy and the external world (Klein, 1952, 1955, p. 141). More recently, developmental psychologists and neuroscientists have argued that such mental capacities cannot be present before at least six months of age (Knox, 2003, pp. 75f.).

Bion, who attended some of Jung's seminars, has a way very similar to Klein's of expressing the process by which a baby has a satisfying experience:

the infant has an inborn disposition corresponding to an expectation of a breast. . . . [T]he preconception (the inborn expectation of a breast, the a priori knowledge of a breast, the 'empty thought') [,] when the infant is brought into contact with the breast itself, mates with the

17

awareness of the realization and is synchronous with the development of a conception. (Bion, 1962, p. 111)

So, both Klein and Bion envisage some sort of structure in the baby at birth, which is not an ego structure, which is psychic and not only physically instinctual, and which mediates the baby's encounter with the external world.

Jung's concept of the archetypes is similarly of a non-ego, innate psychic structure, which governs how we will perceive and respond to our external and internal environment. This idea became central to his understanding of the structure, potential, and development of the total psyche. He developed it gradually, and with many complications and contradictions, over many years from 1912. He saw that, just as we are born with a physical structure adapted for 'a quite definite world where there is water, light, air, salt, carbohydrates', so also we are born with a psychic structure adapted for our psychic environment (Jung, 1928a, p. 190). The archetypes are this structure; they ensure we shall develop psychically as human beings. We share them with all humankind, the dead as well as the living, going back through millennia, in the same way as we share with every person, the dead as well as the living, a bodily structure of bones, organs, nerves. He also emphasized, in contrast to Freud's view, that they are not memory-traces, since they refer not to subject matter but to structure. Despite the early name of 'primordial image', which confusingly seems to imply content, Jung insisted that the archetypes are empty forms, available to shape the universal experience of all people, in every time and in every place – birth, sexuality, death; love and loss; growth and decay; joy and despair. Each archetype holds the opposites – both our instinctual and our non-physical responses to both the hot and the cold, the black and the white, of any experience.

It is argued that Jung's comprehensive theory of archetypes is congruent with current ideas in neuroscience (Knox, 2003). Archetypes are the psychic equivalent of what contemporary neuroscientists describe as neural pathways in our brain: we are born with these structures, but it depends on our life experiences whether or not they will be activated (Pally, 2000, p. 1). If we have a particular experience (such as fear of an angry mother), it has to be registered in one particular neural pathway, which is ready to be activated; similarly, a particular experience has to be registered psychically within its own archetypal structure (in this instance within the archetype of the Terrible Mother). Archetypes are thus one way of thinking about 'mind' in relation to, but distinct from, 'brain'. The profound interlinking between the physical and the psychic is fundamental to archetypal theory and also to neuroscience. Changes in neural pathways have been observed after intensive psychotherapy – it is the intensity of the affect that creates physical changes (Tresan, 1996, p. 416). An understanding of archetypal and neuroscientific theory gives us an immediate way to conceptualize psychosomatic symptoms, in their union of the bodily and the psychic.

The importance of the self

How we view the relations between the self and the ego affects our attitude to our clinical material. Freud thought the ego developed out of the id, as Jung thought it developed out of the unconscious psyche. Freud usually envisaged the id as a constant threat to the ego, though he does mention that 'co-operation' is among the ways the unconscious relates to the conscious psyche (Freud, 1915e: p. 190). He does not note that it has anything useful to contribute. He wrote that the task of the ego was 'taming' the id: to 'master', to 'control', to 'subdue' it (Freud, 1937c, pp. 220–235). Jung had a different view. He thought the unconscious could enrich the ego, if it did not overwhelm it. He wrote about a 'dialogue' between the ego and the unconscious psyche/self in which both parties have 'equal rights' (Jung, 1957, p. 89). He thought the aim of psychic development was not that the ego should 'master' the unconscious psyche, but that it should acknowledge the power of the self and consider accommodating its own actions to the needs and wishes of its unconscious partner. He thought that the self has a wisdom beyond our merely individual ego-understanding, in that one self is connected to all other human (and perhaps non-human) selves.

For Freud, the ego is, in psychic health, the dominant force in the psyche. 'Psychoanalytic treatment,' he writes, 'is based upon an influencing of the *Ucs.* from the direction of the *Cs.*' (Freud, 1915e, p. 194; original italics). An unconscious activity that enters consciousness acts, he says, as a 'reinforcement' of the activity intended by the ego. This co-operation can only happen when the energy from the unconscious can be transformed into an ego-syntonic energy. For Jung, the emphasis is reversed. Analysis is based on an influencing of the conscious psyche from the direction of the unconscious, so that consciousness can become more full and more complete. The ego's attitude is not reinforced but modified, or its bias is compensated, by the unconscious attitude. A third position is constellated, something new, previously unknown, unimaginable to the ego on its own (Jung, 1957, p. 90). Moreover, for Freud the initiative lies with the ego, even if unconsciously – the activity is 'intended' by the ego. For Jung, the initiative lies with the self, 'wanting' to be realized.

For Jung, the self is primary: it is there first: out of it emerges the ego. As Fordham develops Jung's ideas, the primary self of the infant is our original psychosomatic unity, which gradually differentiates into psyche and soma as the ego grows. The self is also primary for Jung in the sense that there is more of it than there is of the ego and that it continuously, throughout life, supplies the psychic creativity that we experience in our dreams (with their newly minted images each night), our poems, our solutions to scientific conundrums. It seems inexhaustible – though since we can only ever know of it what becomes conscious, we can never know its full extent or capacities. Yet our experience is that it rules our life – it is the needs, wishes and intentions of our self (to speak anthropomorphically, and perhaps accurately) that govern the shape our life will take: what we will do, whom we will marry (or not), often what illnesses we will suffer from and even, sometimes, when and how we will die. As in chaos theory in modern physics, the apparent randomness of our life disguises a deeper pattern and purpose.

Freud regarded the analyst as a detective, trying to track down a criminal, and using manifestations from the unconscious psyche as clues (Freud, 1916–1917, p. 51). This is markedly different from Jung's attitude, which regarded all clinical material – dreams, psychosomatic suffering, enactments, pathological (neurotic/psychotic) symptoms, transference and countertransference phenomena – as 'angels': that is, as messengers from the unconscious psyche, 'trying' to get a message through to conscious awareness. He thought that it is our job to help the patient integrate into their consciousness whatever the content and the meanings of these messages might be, so that the messengers can go off duty: 'message received'.

Jung often speaks anthropomorphically of 'the self', as if it is a personality within our unconscious psyche that has wants and purposes of its own. It is, he says, 'so to speak, a personality which we *also* are (Jung, 1928a, p. 177; original italics). He tries to distinguish from a 'second ego' what such an 'unconscious' personality might be like – perhaps 'dormant' or 'dreaming' (Jung, 1939, pp. 282f.). In practice, we cannot distinguish what might be the instinctual, impersonal 'drive' of an archetype (or from the id) from the intentional 'want' of a subject that is unconscious. But it makes a difference to our clinical attitude, and probably to our clinical practice, if we agree with Jung, as he writes in the same passage:

The collaboration of the unconscious [with consciousness] is intelligent and purposive, and even when it acts in opposition to consciousness its expression is still compensatory in an intelligent way, as if it were trying to restore the lost balance. (*ibid.*, p. 281)

To think of our non-conscious psyche in this way means we are listening, as it were, to another person, and we are expecting them to be purposeful, intelligent and compensatory of the conscious attitude. They may cause trouble, but we are not expecting them to be solely a trouble-maker.

Jung's archetype of the self

After his break with Freud in 1912, Jung entered a time of deliberate, conscious co-operation with what he felt as huge pressure from his unconscious psyche (which he was not then thinking of as his 'self'). This phase culminated in a dream, in 1927, of being in Liverpool with a companion. He writes:

> [W]e found a broad square dimly illuminated by street lights, into which many streets converged. The various quarters of the city were arranged radially around the square. In the centre was a round pool, and in the middle of it a small island. While everything round about was obscured by rain, fog, smoke, and dimly lit darkness, the little island blazed with sunlight. On it stood a single tree, a magnolia, in a shower of reddish blossoms. It was as though the tree stood in the sunlight and was at the same time the source of light. (Jung, 1962, p. 223)

Jung comments:

> This dream represented my situation at the time. I can still see the greyish-yellow raincoats, glistening with the wetness of the rain. Everything was extremely unpleasant, black and opaque – just as I felt then. But I had had a vision of unearthly beauty, and that was why I was able to live at all. (*ibid.*, p. 224)

He had understood that, for him, '[t]he centre is the goal, and everything is directed towards that centre'; the centre is the self, and 'the self is the principle and archetype of orientation and meaning'. Out of this experience emerged 'a first inkling of my personal myth', of the psychic process towards individuation (*ibid.*).

The archetype of the self is an organizing principle whose function is to integrate, unify, pull towards a centre, all the infinite potentialities within the whole psyche, and so to bring about a state of greater psychic wholeness. Later writers have noted that Jung's theory of archetypes indicates that the archetype of the self will also include the opposite pole – a predisposition for psychic entities to disintegrate, fight, or stagnate. Two contemporary Jungian analysts have explored this: Redfearn in his book *The Exploding Self* (1992) and Gordon in her consideration of how the tendency to unity can itself become damaging, if it is so strong that it totally prevents de-integration, differentiation, separation (Gordon, 1985, pp. 268f.). These explorations warn us not to idealize the archetype of the self as a centring principle, or the aim of psychotherapy as calm and orderly wholeness. Hillman's preference for a polytheistic, rather than a monotheistic, view of the structure of the psyche also encourages us to value the diversity of our internal world, and not necessarily to expect an over-arching order (Hillman, 1976, p. 35).

Jung devotes a whole chapter of *Aion* (1951, pp. 222–265) to listing, detailing, and considering a cornucopia of symbols for the self. Because it is an archetype, and therefore an empty structure, any image can express only a limited amount of the total potential of this structure; we each approach this potential with images from our own experience, and so our archetypal experience becomes personalized, and is brought within the human sphere. A particular named experience/individual is incarnated/comes into existence in a particular moment of time: such as, Jesus is born as the son of God.

The 'God-language' provides links, for those to whom it is meaningful, between the theories of depth psychology and other important areas of human experience. It gives us a way of understanding clinically the language and problems of those patients who are deeply distressed by their relationship to their 'God', a way that is not limited to thinking of their 'God' as just an internal object built up according to Kleinian theory. Black (1993) suggests a variant on this Kleinian model for the existence of our internal God.

Individuation

Jung often uses the image of the spiral: as we walk in our ego round our self, we get nearer to the centre, meeting again and again, in different contexts and with different emphases, our core self. We find this frequently in clinical practice: an image a patient brings in the first session may contain the focus of all the work we do.

'Individuation' is about becoming more conscious of who we are. Jung defines it in 1928:

> Individuation means becoming an 'in-dividual,' and, in so far as 'individuality' embraces our innermost, last, and incomparable uniqueness, it also implies becoming one's own self. We could therefore translate individuation as 'coming to selfhood' or 'self-realization.' (Jung, 1928a, p. 173)

Previously ignored or conflictual aspects of our self are brought into our consciousness; communication is established. We become no longer a house divided against itself; we are undivided, in-dividual. Our self becomes real, has an actual rather than a potential existence. It exists in reality, enacted in the real world; it is 'realized', as we say an idea is 'realized' when it is accomplished. Jung writes: 'The psyche is an equation that cannot be "solved" without the factor of the unconscious; it is a totality which includes both the empirical ego and its transconscious foundation' (Jung 1955–1956, p. 155).

The process of individuation is the work of solving this equation. It is never completed.

CHAPTER THREE

SUB-PERSONALITIES AND INTERNAL OBJECTS

'The united personality will never quite lose
the painful sense of innate discord'
(Jung, 1946, p. 200)

The drama of our psychic life, as Jungian theory understands it, consists in the developing relationship between
our self and our ego – urgent or stagnant, stormy or
harmonious, now self, now ego leading the way.
Communication between the self and the ego can consist
of a reasonably civilized dialogue, a squabble, a full-blown
row, an invasion, or a tyrannical oppression. One party
may try to ignore the other entirely. Later chapters will
consider these various manifestations.

Within the self there is also a cast of characters who,
like swimmers with their heads above water, are partly in
consciousness and partly not. These are the internal
objects of the object-relations school, the complexes or
sub-personalities in Jungian theory. They are like a family
or community living together, or like the characters in a
play: total agreement is impossible, because different
people want different things. There is 'innate discord'.
This experience is symbolized in the pantheon of gods on
Mount Olympus, the many inter-related gods of Hindu
theology, and the varied saints in the Christian tradition.

Our task as clinicians is not to arbitrate between these conflicting claims, though we are often tempted to do so. Our task is to help our patients differentiate their ego, as well as their sense of their own self, from an identification with any of the participants. The patient comes to recognize that he or she is the author of the story, the writer of the drama, and even though this particular cast of characters is by now a 'given', patients have some say in how the story-line will develop. Their say will never be absolute or unconditional – not only is the power of past experiences being enacted, but the self may introduce new characters as external or internal circumstances change and the opportunity arises for a new aspect of the total personality to enter consciousness and be integrated into the person's experience of themselves. It makes a difference to the clinician whether she regards this new development as primarily an opportunity or primarily as trouble. It will, of course, always be both.

In the story of Snow White, for instance, envy is activated only when the girl begins to grow up: the good mother, who died when the child was born and so leaves the story, is replaced by a step-mother, narcissistically preoccupied only with her own image in the mirror (and not, therefore, paying attention to, or 'mirroring', the young child); and when Snow White reaches the age of seven, this Queen becomes envious. The story tells us that when this developmental stage is reached it gives the girl the opportunity to learn about the envy and rivalry between herself and her mother, and to face and cope with her own envious feelings. The envious step-mother-Queen enters the child's internal story, and the story-line has to adapt to include her; but the child has some say in how it adapts.

Internal objects and internal people

Meeting the term 'internal objects' to describe the living and passionate experience of our internal reality is usually a shock. It seems an odd and impersonal way to describe our experience of other people. It implies we are objective about our 'objects'. Freud used the term 'object' to denote the object of a person's desire – usually a person or part of a person; Klein developed the concept of 'internal objects' in great detail, and studied how their relation to one another created the subject's total psychic structure. Jung refers rather to 'imagoes' (as also does Klein) or, more frequently, to *complexes*, which he thinks of as splinter psyches. Each complex is part conscious, part unconscious, part archetypal, part personal, an autonomous cluster of images and ideas round one particular emotional tone.

It is a common experience that the life of the imagination – the fantasy life of our internal world – has a life of its own: as many novelists say, they don't know beforehand how the story will turn out; it seems that their characters 'take over'. Jung's style of writing, which infuriates some readers, reflects his own similar experience – that he could meet 'people' (such as Philemon – see Chapter One) in the world of his imagination who had their own autonomous lives. He (his ego) was not controlling when they appeared or what they thought or said. Consequently, he writes:

> in describing the living processes of the psyche, I deliberately and consciously give preference to a dramatic, mythological way of thinking and speaking, because this is not only more expressive but also more exact than an abstract scientific terminology. (Jung, 1951, p. 13)

29

This understanding, that the psyche is, *exactly*, 'dramatic' – that is, like a drama, like people interacting with each other – is useful clinically because it can help the therapist to work more from her right brain, imaginatively, than from her left, more analytic, brain. This frees her to access other, associated stories – myths, fairytales, novels, films – to amplify, and so to help her understand, the patient's internal story.

And it is the patient's internal story, their largely unconscious story, that is the focus of our clinical attention.

Mythological amplification: Anna/Electra

Anna was an unmarried woman patient of nearly forty who was desperate to have children. Her childhood had been dominated by absent parents – her father often physically away, travelling for his work, and her mother physically present but emotionally absent, depressed, and narcissistic. Father at home was the highlight of her life; she remembered him as warm and tender towards her, and encouraging her in her academic pursuits. Father had retired some five years previously, and shortly afterwards had died, not enjoying the retirement with her mother that he had planned. Anna had huge resentment towards her mother for being alive when her father was dead. She idealized her dead father, and denigrated her living mother. Thus she kept both parents still, internally, absent to her. She was stuck in deep mourning for her father.

We can think of this material in many object-relation ways. Anna has identified with a dead internal object; the dead father has activated her early mourning for the loss of her 'good' mother; she has lost her good internal object with the loss of her good external object; she has lost her good internal object because her own internal persecutory objects have destroyed it; Anna has no good internal parental couple with which she can identify in a fruitful union of her own; she is still bound Oedipally to her dead father and so is not free to leave her mourning and seek a partner of her own; she fears to triumph over her mother by leaving her mother for a husband and by having a more successful marriage than her mother; her conscious longing for children hides an unconscious fear of being a mother, perhaps from fear of rivalry with her own mother –and so on (cf. Freud, 1917e, pp. 243–258; Klein, 1940, pp. 345–355; Winnicott, 1950). All these ideas are pertinent and potentially useful.

But her therapist's main experience of being with Anna was that Anna experienced herself as a helpless victim of fate, and was waiting for him to rescue her. An object-relations approach would suggest exploration of the victim–oppressor–rescuer (absent) triad, and the therapist might have considered work by Rosenfeld, who writes of the dream of a patient he calls Simon (Rosenfeld, 1987, p. 110). Simon is standing watching a dying boy lying in the hot midday sun, and is doing nothing to help him, but is critical of the doctor not moving the boy into the shade. But Anna's therapist thought also of the story of Electra.

Electra was the middle daughter of Agamemnon and Clytemnestra (so Aeschylus, Sophocles, and Euripides tell us). Agamemnon tricked Clytemnestra into bringing their elder daughter, Iphigenia, to Aulis, with the promise of marriage to a Grecian prince, Achilles. Agamemnon's fleet was marooned on Aulis, waiting for winds favourable to waft them to Troy to take revenge for the Trojan abduction of Clytemnestra's sister, Helen. Agamemnon had

previously offended the goddess Artemis by killing a preg-
nant hare, and she required him to sacrifice Iphigenia to
obtain the wind he needed – his daughter, in compensation for the dead leverets. So Agamemnon killed his
daughter, the wind changed, and he set sail for Troy.
Clytemnestra, furious and grieving, took a lover,
Aegisthus, during the army's ten-year absence, and
Electra, a grievous reminder to Clytemnestra of her other,
dead, daughter and her treacherous husband, was
banished from court to live with peasants (in one version,
she was married to a peasant, so that if she had a child
it would be of base blood and so could not inherit the
kingdom). When, ten years later, Agamemnon returned
home as the great victor, flaunting his mistress Cassandra,
Clytemnestra slew him in his welcome-home bath. Electra
smuggled her ten-year-old brother, Orestes, out of the
city. She passed her days in misery and lamentation,
particularly at her father's tomb. She idealized her father,
and was waiting for Orestes to become a grown man and
revenge her father's murder by killing her mother. She
could not act without a man.

Her therapist thought of all the characters in the story
as being potentially aspects of Anna's psyche – and
currently, clearly, Anna was identified with Electra. He
did not refer to the story in the sessions; it was a silent countertransference association, or amplification. He was struck
by the fact that Electra is waiting to be rescued by her
brother, Orestes, hidden just before puberty; when he
returns as a man he will free Electra from her bondage to
her father, and he will kill the bad-mother part of her that
was keeping her as a thrall and preventing her having
children and taking her rightful place in the world. This
led to exploration of the transference to him (as Orestes):

idealized, a potential but inept (immature) saviour and, hence, persecutory (withholding). As well as this work in the transference the therapist began to explore with Anna what she might think of as 'masculine' in her psyche, but which was missing, or dead (brother, father). They considered how Anna might also be identified with and, therefore, enacting the part of, Clytemnestra-mother, a violent, life-denying person. The fact that both parents in the story deny their daughters the right to life and children brought the Oedipal tangle in Anna's life into vivid prominence in her therapist's mind. He wondered whether these parents might represent an unconscious fear in Anna of having children, compensatory to her conscious longing for them. Were these the literal, externally real children that Anna wanted, or did they also symbolize Anna's own child-self: her potential for growth and development, her vulnerability, her longing to find the 'good' mother she had missed in childhood, her longing to be dependent? Was she afraid not only of growing up and facing her Oedipal dilemmas, but also of regression to dependence?

This therapist used the story of Electra to open up possible ways of thinking with Anna about her material and the object relations issues that were keeping her from developing.

The formation of internal objects: innate, *a priori*, archetypal

There is broad agreement as to how these internal people develop in each of us individually. Klein's unconscious phantasy and Bion's pre-conception, like Jung's archetypal expectation (see Chapter One), all meet with external reality: the mother as she really is, the feed that does or doesn't go well. It is the combination of the internal expectation (the same in us all) and the external reality (different for each of us) that forms the internal object. Yet, it is not so simple. Even the internal expectation may vary according to 'personal disposition' – the 'innate factor' (Bion, 1959, p. 105; Britton, 1998, p. 58), which may be particular differences in brain structure at birth, leading to potentially different emphases in psychic development. There is also a different emphasis in different theorists as to whether internal expectation or external reality has more influence – Klein emphasizes more the universal role of unconscious phantasy and so emphasizes such features as the oral sadism of all babies; whereas Winnicott and Kohut counteract this bias with an emphasis on the actual maternal environment (Winnicott, 1960b, p. 38; Siegel, 1996, pp. 30f.). But Klein also writes of the importance of the actual mother (Klein, 1940, p. 346) and Winnicott also writes of the importance of the infant's unconscious phantasies (of going to pieces, falling for ever, etc.) (Winnicott, 1962, pp. 57f.; for Kohut see Siegel, 1996, pp. 34f.).

Jung notes that in an adult there is a gradation between the images of internal objects that are totally archetypal and those that are totally human. An archetypal image of mother, for instance, would operate totally unconsciously and might lead to the ego identifying with either the All-Providing or All-Devouring mother. Many compulsive 'helpers' are unconsciously identified with their internal image of the archetype of the All-Providing mother: it is unattainable, unrealistic, inhuman, and hence they are always failing and bound to compulsive repetition. Many patients project this image on to their therapist, who will also inevitably fail to live up to the image of superhuman care. The therapeutic task is to enable the patient to discover and accept the terrible, infuriating reality that the therapist's failure to be perfect, and so to disappoint, is not a total disaster. The patient's archetypal image (or ego-ideal) thus gradually also becomes more human and less persecutory. Redfearn gives an example: the image of a volcano to express a person's rage may become modified later in the therapy to that of a dangerous animal, and later still to that of an angry person (Redfearn, 1992, p. 20).

To be able to monitor our patients' internal images as somewhere along the archetypal–human continuum can help us clinically – to discern, for instance, how much of their response to an unexpected absence or a suggested fee rise is located in objective reality and how much it needs meeting at the level of primitive terror or rage.

Most clinicians have faced a patient whose history seems so terrible that it is impossible to locate any external person who could have helped to form a good internal object. Yet, the patient clearly has something good: they have come to therapy, which indicates that they have hope; they may be (quite often) a good mother or faithful in a caring capacity to a person or animal who is dependent on them. The therapist may cast around for a grandmother, school teacher, uncle, even a friendly person in the local newsagent's – some external person who could, however briefly, have given the child an experience of hope of someone solid, steady, loving. Then the theoretical dynamic can be fulfilled – the unconscious phantasy/archetypal expectation meets with external reality and so an internal object is formed.

Kalsched, however, argues that within our archetypal structures, in the collective unconscious and quite distinct from any personal experience, there are *pre-existing images* of figures that can provide a 'self-care system' for the profoundly distressed human soul. When someone has split off from an unbearably traumatic experience, an archetypal figure may receive and minister to them. Such figures are imaged as angels in the Judaic and Christian tradition. Kalsched has a particular phrase for these figures that captures their essential archetypal bi-polar nature; he calls them Protector–Persecutors (Kalsched, 1998, p. 4). This figure is akin to Rosenfeld's concept of a type of narcissism which 'often acts as an essential protector of the self' (Rosenfeld, 1987, p. 105).

Sub-personalities: internal and external communication: Barbara

A patient, Barbara, middle-aged and married, used her experience in therapy to modify her archetypal images and to integrate more of her sub-personalities into her ego. Communication, both external and internal, improved as a result of the analysis of her relationship with her therapist. Despite having a well-functioning ego, which enabled her to live a well-adapted and externally success-ful life most of the time, in her early sessions she regressed to a state where her sense of 'I' was identified with a trau-matized, undeveloped part of her self, which could not speak. This terrified person was kept safe, but in prison (or psychic death) by her 'Protector–Persecutor', whose message was, 'Stay away from reality, so that you won't ever get hurt again' (Kalsched, 1996, pp. 4f.).

At first, her 'Protector–Persecutor' took the image of a boa-constrictor, which she experienced as winding itself round her body, crushing the breath out of her. She felt the waves of constriction passing down her body, and the physical impediment was effective – she could not speak. Sometimes she said nothing at all for half an hour, or hid completely under her coat – dominated by this figure from her unconscious psyche. But Barbara was not psychotic; she knew there was no boa-constrictor in the room, and this behaviour gradually ceased. The prevalent image changed to that of being in a bunker: she packed the cushions round her and used them, and the arm of the chair, consciously to enact a physical protection against the therapist. She became able to put into words what had before been unconscious and therefore 'silent'; she could now say, 'I don't want to talk to you', or 'I don't want to tell you anything'.

An interesting conceptualization of Barbara's 'bunker mentality' is offered by Steiner. He identified a particular defensive 'place' of no movement, between and separate from the paranoid–schizoid and depressive positions, which he called a 'psychic retreat' (cf. Steiner, 1993). The purpose of this no-feeling place is to avoid painful experiences of loss. Barbara had split off and denied some aspects of herself, but in the bunker she was protected from knowing about them or mourning her lost selves (sub-personalities).

Gradually the denial became less total. 'If I let you in so that you know me, you won't like me,' she said from time to time. This expressed her fear that if bunker-Barbara were reached by her other 'selves', 'she' would not like 'them', nor 'they' like 'her'. This fear modified over time, and she became more likely to say, 'I don't know what to say', or 'I don't know how to begin', or 'My mind's a blank'. Her 'I' had shifted. She was no longer identified only with the terrified person in the bunker, but also with a person who might like to talk but finds it difficult

During this time, she lined up on the couch a row of imaginary children – one made from corrugated cardboard, one screaming, one asleep, one with long fair hair, one solemnly sucking her thumb. These sad, desperate, internal children were the unlikely troops she had feared would assault her in her bunker. She realized that she had been identified with the cardboard cut-out person, a two-dimensional figure, but now, in becoming more aware of the three-dimensionality of her body, she suffered many psychosomatic symptoms. She also found that she identified with others of the children – for a while she sucked her thumb in the sessions, and spoke very little; later, she cried throughout most of her sessions for many months. It became possible, through the mediation of the therapist's mind, for these internal people to talk to the therapist, to each other, and to Barbara's ego.

Patients are often aware of some degree of discord or of poor communication between their sub-personalities, with inconsistent and disturbing identifications. The therapist's experience of Barbara was also very varied – that her ego-identity had not quite settled. She seemed now very large, now quite small, now fragile, now tough, now unreachable, now forcing her way into him. Barbara brought to her sessions for many months, before and after her experience of her row of children, accounts of meetings where people found it difficult to express themselves, or to hear or to understand others – a description of her own inner world. It was a sign of increasing psychic integration when Barbara could recognize that all these people were representing different aspects of her self – and even to see this not as dreadful ('I couldn't wear shocking pink like that woman does!') but as a sign of her own inner richness – that she too could have the freedom to wear bright colours, to *be* 'bright', and even shocking. This was a far step from her conscious identification with the cardboard cut-out child.

Sub-personalities: internal and external communication: Catherine

Another patient, Catherine, a single woman in her thirties, had experienced great difficulty in several short-term and painful relationships. She came into therapy hoping for help in forming a lasting partnership. Her therapist discovered that the different aspects of Catherine's psyche were represented by images of broken-down machines – a bike, a car – by lengths of pipe waiting to be connected in road works, or by a tangle of wires at the telephone exchange. These impersonal, mechanical images suggested functions, or qualities: they were nearer the archetypal than the human end of the continuum. This informed her therapist that Catherine had developed the symbolic capacity (image-making) that is a necessary precursor to relating to people as separate objects. However, the non-human character of her images indicated that Catherine's experience of her sub-personalities was less personalized than Barbara's had become, whose images were of people – people at meetings, or the various children. Therefore transference interpretations, or attempts to think about the meaning of how she was with the therapist, might well arouse incomprehension, fear, and hostility.

After some time in therapy, Catherine spoke of failed attempts at communication: post arriving after she had left home; her answerphone not recording a message; a child missing a ball she was trying to kick and dropping a ball she was trying to catch. Although these images all illustrated communications that failed, and left her feeling empty and lonely, there were at last people implied or present in her images. Therapist and patient could together understand that as well as the pain of 'missing', these images showed some hope, some expectation that it was possible to make the attempt to relate. The fact that they were making this understanding together both facilitated and exemplified Catherine's whole psychic process. Catherine and her therapist were learning to 'play ball' together and it was now possible to interpret the transference between himself and Catherine, as well as the relationship between different aspects of her self.

Multiple personalities

These dissociated sub-personalities exemplify a 'vertical splitting' of the self (cf. Robinson & Fuller, 2003, p. 71). This can range from the mild form frequently experienced as '"I" don't like "myself" today', to extreme pathological dissociation where the separate personalities lead (from the patient's point of view) quite separate lives and have no knowledge of what the other personalities do. This used to be known as multiple personality disorder, and has been the subject of media attention because of its dramatic potential. When there is then no coherent, over-arching sense of 'myself', one of these 'people' may come into consciousness, like waking up, with a terrified sense of having 'lost' three hours, or three days (cf. Everest, 1999). Recently, this state has been redesignated

Dissociative Identity Disorder, which is a better term because it takes account of the defensive function of the symptoms. It is increasingly thought that the disorder can be associated with traumatic childhood abuse.

Non-ego voices and psychosomatic messages

There is a spectrum of psychological disturbance in people who hear voices; a patient who hears voices is not necessarily psychotic. It is the degree of the dissociation we need to assess: can the patient think about the existence and location of their voices, as well as about the content of what the voices say? A patient who shows, by their ability to think about these phenomena, that their ego is still reasonably strong and functioning, can be helped to understand the voices as expressing the points of view of different sub-personalities.

This would not be advisable or even possible for a patient who does not have an ego-position separate from the voices. When the unconscious psyche is dominating their ego, people project the archetypal figures so powerfully that they become convinced that the voices they hear come from aliens or other people or demons in the television. This phenomenon is unfortunately well-documented in tragic newspaper reports of (usually) young schizophrenic men who have heard, and obeyed, the voice of God telling them to kill the devil in themselves, or in their parents, or in a particular stranger in the street. Such patients need psychiatric treatment and possibly physical containment as a priority over psychotherapy. Their psychological reality is acknowledged in criminal law, as manifested in the defences of 'diminished responsibility' and 'insanity'.

Other people may hear voices from God but they retain also a well-functioning ego. Joan of Arc, a young French peasant woman in the fourteenth century, is a famous example. She heard angels' voices in the church bells telling her to go to the Dauphin (the uncrowned French king), raise an army, and expel the occupying English forces from her native land. The story tells that she thought about these voices for some time, then had to test the external reality of their message against other people's reactions to the possibility of expelling the English, before she could eventually get to the Dauphin and subsequently lead the army. Joan's voices were regarded as 'good' by her compatriots but not, of course, by the English.

Sometimes the psyche 'uses' the body to try to get a vital message into consciousness: as with Barbara there may be a psychosomatic illness, or there may be an accident. Jung's assertion that 'the unconscious is the psyche of all the body's autonomous functional complexes' (Jung, 1941, p. 172) gives us a conceptual framework for understanding such dangers. Diseases of the immune system, for example, where the body enacts what may well be a murderous psychic attack on the person's very existence, can be related to a self-hating, self-destructive sub-personality denied other means of expression. We might think of it as an enactment of suicidal impulses. Some such patients can be helped through intensive psychotherapy although only rarely is the psychological element to such illnesses fully recognized and the sufferers offered any psychological help. But for other patients the risk of psychic death (madness) is as great as, or greater than, the risk of physical death, and so psychological insight must be rejected in favour of staying with the concrete physical symptoms.

Non-ego voices: Donna

The emergence of a hidden sub-personality can happen quite suddenly in a session. Donna, a young and ambitious woman, was talking about a current task at work when her voice suddenly changed and she said, 'I don't want to!' She looked startled, broke off and asked, 'Where did that come from?' looking round as if she expected to see someone sitting next to her. She and her therapist identified this new voice as belonging to a little girl in her, who found the pressures of adult life sometimes too much and who currently tried to get cared for through the physical problems that occasionally kept her off work for a few days, and through the constant arguments with her partner about who was responsible for doing the shopping or the ironing. Donna became quite fond of this child, consciously imagined her sitting next to her on the couch, put her arm round her and comforted her. She had indeed as a child often carried what she had experienced as too great responsibilities, in being 'the little mother' to younger siblings when her mother was incapacitated through depression. In place of her unconscious rage over the loss of a carefree childhood, expressed in her rage at being currently 'over'-worked, she could now, in the therapy, develop a conscious, present relationship with this still-living aspect of her total psyche, symbolized in her overburdened, protesting child-self. Her working, responsible adult could now give this 'child' consideration and comfort, and could begin to co-operate in discussion with her partner about the allocation of household jobs and to renegotiate some of her work load. What had been 'conflict' had become some degree of 'collaboration'.

Who am 'I'?

There is always some dissociation. We cannot or do not want to acknowledge our envy, bad temper, or longing for love as part of our sense of identity. Hence such common phrases as 'I'm not myself today', or 'I was beside myself with rage' (the rage neatly placed 'beside' rather than 'within' 'myself'). These phrases imply a potential state of psychic harmony, which is currently absent, when I *am* 'myself'. They refer to a sense of coherent personal identity and in this they relate to the 'self' of Freud and of Kohut.

There can also be great relief when 'I' is differentiated from a particular sub-personality. One patient realized that it was not himself, but his internal mother, who was saying he was a failure, and, as he put it, 'I can talk to her – I'm bigger than she is.' Another patient also learned to say, 'I can make a mistake.' She knew that this was not the same as her previous experience, that 'I am a failure.' 'I' has become an ego that can do things, make things, relate to the world sometimes well and sometimes not so well. It has become differentiated from her self, which continues even if 'I' make a mistake.

CHAPTER FOUR

THE SELF–EGO RELATIONSHIP IN INFANCY AND CHILDHOOD

'Just as a man still is what he always was,
so he already is what he will become'
(Jung, 1940–1941, p. 258)

The self as innate potential

When a baby is born, her body is already programmed by its collective genetic inheritance to have a human skeletal and organic structure. It is also programmed by personal genetic inheritance, so that, if circumstances are favourable, she will develop the family's bigger or smaller bones, the taller or shorter stature, that she is designed for. Deprivation, accident, illness, or warfare can affect this programme; but it is already set.

At birth, her psyche is similarly already programmed by its collective and familial inheritance. The detailed psychic development of any individual will depend on particular environmental experiences interacting with personal psychological characteristics. We do not yet know exactly how one relates to the other. One possibility is that mind/ psyche is a manifestation solely of brain. This theory would explain how the psyches of identical twins are not identical. We can think that each brain developed differently in infancy, because of the inevitable environmental differences even when the twins are brought up together. The differences between their adult psyches are then physical (in the brain) but not genetic; they are due to nurture, not nature.

Because theorists have used the term, 'the self', differently, it is difficult to compare their views on the newly born. Although more recent psychoanalytic concepts of the self regard it as a vital agent in psychic development (Kohut and Fonagy, for example, see Chapter Two), the psychoanalytic 'self' has not traditionally been considered to be present at birth, coming into existence only when the developing ego could become conscious of itself – when a capacity for objectivity developed.

Jung's approach is different. He envisages that a person's full self, in potential, is in her at birth. This 'primary self' (Fordham, 1973, p. 84) seems a totally different entity from that supposed by other theorists. A huge cast of characters is seen as sitting around the empty stage in the shadows; some will have no part to play; others will have leading roles. But they are all already there, waiting their opportunity.

The work of developmental psychologists has helped us to a greater understanding of the infant's experience than was available to earlier theoreticians – and so perhaps to more accurate theoretical formulations. Daniel Stern, a psychiatrist specializing in infant development, suggests that an infant develops a sense of a 'core self' between two and seven months. He emphasizes that this is not a cognitive construct, nor an awareness of a self: it is an 'experiential integration' of a sense of self-agency, self-coherence, self-affectivity and self-history (Stern 1985, p. 71), all terms that in most theories are linked to ego-function.

The undifferentiated primary self

In psychoanalytic theory, a newborn's psyche is at an 'undifferentiated stage of development when one may say that all is sensory experience' (Milrod, 2002, p. 10, citing Hartmann). Winnicott similarly postulates 'a primary unintegration' (Winnicott, 1945, p. 149). Klein, on the other hand, held that 'from the beginning of post-natal life' the infant mind has an ego that continuously experiences an 'inner life' as well as 'the outer world', and is subject to mechanisms of splitting, projection and introjection 'from birth onwards' (Klein, 1959, p. 250). However, current thinking by neuroscientists and developmental psychologists suggests that the baby is not capable of forming internal objects until after six months (Knox, 2003, pp. 75f.).

Fordham postulates that in the primary self there is at times no distinction between consciousness and unconsciousness, between the psyche and the body, between the ego and the self, between me and not-me, between my self and an other, between inside and outside (Fordham, 1973, pp. 85–87; cf. Astor, 1995, pp. 53f.). The skin is not in this state experienced as a boundary: taking in by feeding and pushing out by excreting are not connected with an awareness of inside and outside. Although there is no 'inner world', only sensory experiences of pleasure or discomfort, such sensations are represented mentally by emotions, or primitive feelings. With experiences come images: the Jungian neonatal self contains the psychic structure of all the archetypes but these remain undifferentiated until the baby has experiences that 'meet' them. The archetypal potential is then real-ized as images that form the basis of consciousness. Imagery arises only through experience.

As the baby encounters her environment and begins to differentiate one object from another, one person from another, one feeling from another, this primary self unfolds and loses its original undifferentiated unity. Some of its unconscious contents are differentiated in consciousness, and soma and psyche also become more distinct: the body no longer has to cope unaided with psychic phenomena to the same extent. In Winnicott's phrase, 'the psyche has come to live in the soma' (Winnicott, 1962, p. 61).

The devastating effects of sensory deprivation at this stage of development are highlighted by a cruel experiment in which two kittens were only briefly exposed to light each day. Both were kept in baskets and deprived of touch, but in the light one kitten could just reach the ground with its paws, and so move its basket round in a circle. It was discovered that this kitten developed sight, but the other was totally blind. Something crucial in the passive, non-touching, kitten's brain did not develop: a capacity to perceive external phenomena, a capacity to link its perception with some form of understanding, or a capacity to communicate (Gregory, 1966, pp. 211f.).

Differentiation: mother and baby

Observations of babies with their mothers, and tests of the sensory and cognitive capacities of very young babies, have shown that complex processes of observation, integration, memory, and adaptation, are certainly present from birth. As long ago as 1987, Chamberlain noted that it was not any longer possible to consider a newborn infant other than as 'well-equipped, sentient, communicative,

attentive, able to pick up and integrate complex informa-
tion, and to make personal adjustments to the environment' (Chamberlain, 1987, p. 30). Such an infant is
clearly a being separate from her mother, communicating
with many aspects of her environment, both personal and
material.

Some theoreticians would call these skills signs of the
functioning of the ego, some of the functioning of the
self. As Fordham writes in 1973:

> Either [the baby] starts from a primarily unorganized
> state or there are organized archetypal patterns inbuilt
> and ready to become activated. Those who think a baby's
> energies are essentially unorganized will attribute any
> organized activities that he reveals to the ego; those, like
> myself, who approach the subject with Jung's concepts in
> mind, will contend that a baby's archetypal patterns are
> more likely to be finding expression in organized behavi-
> our which will not necessarily be attributed to the ego.
> (Fordham, 1973, pp. 88f.)

Experimental psychologists have recorded observations
of babies only a few days old imitating someone sticking
their tongue out. This is a complicated matter: it involves
recognizing a face as like their own face, recognizing a
tongue by sight, and transferring that recognition from
sight across the modes of perception to sensation so the
tongue they see is identified with the tongue inside their
own mouth that they can feel. The babies know which
muscles to use to make their tongue stick out in the same
way as the tongue they are looking at sticks out. It is an
amazingly complex and co-ordinated response (Meltzoff
& Moore, 1977, cited in Chamberlain, 1987, p. 45).
Studies of infants still in the womb showing continuity

between pre- and post-natal physical and personality traits, suggest that the embryonic baby may already experience the uterine environment as 'other' and so begin mental development through interaction with the environment of the womb (Piontelli, 1992).

Mothers certainly know that their babies are separately existing individuals, and relate to them as if the baby has an ongoing self that is recognizably the same over time and through different moods. They recognize the different selves of their different babies. We know that, from immediately after birth, mother and baby are trying to make a relationship.

Unconscious identity: a regressive longing

There is a persistent human fantasy of longed-for total oneness with another. This is most commonly felt by adult lovers: that they are 'at one' or 'as one'. These experiences may in part be attributable to a projection on to the other person of our remembered experience of our own selves in the womb or in a state of primary unity, when there was no separation between our conscious and our unconscious psyche: we become again unconscious, without all the upheaval, work, responsibility and conflict that a separate ego entails.

Freud seems to be writing of this experience when he refers to the psychological cocoon surrounding the baby's fragile narcissism with the 'oceanic feeling' of 'a bond with the universe' (Freud, 1930a, pp. 64–73). Jung, similarly, thought that at first the baby is in a state of 'unconscious identity' with her parents, that 'fusion with the psychology of the parents' is her normal, ongoing experience (Jung, 1928b, pp. 53, 56). In this state there is nothing to filter the flow of feelings and phantasies from one person to another. Winnicott writes of the infant as, at first, 'merged' with the mother (Winnicott, 1960b, p. 50), Mahler and colleagues of a 'normal' 'symbiotic phase' (a 'self-object undifferentiated state') out of which the baby 'hatches' (Mahler, Pine, & Bergman, 1975, pp. 8–9), and Neumann of 'the extra-uterine embryonic stage' (Neumann, 1973, p. 13). Despite the evidence of a newborn baby having quite sophisticated capacities, these theories are still often taught and included in publications.

Myths of all cultures seem to include a reference to an idyllic state of being, set far in the past. In Chinese myth there is the triumvirate of ideal (male) rulers in the Golden Age of Antiquity, when government was founded on moral values. There is the Dreamtime of the Aboriginal people of Australia, the Golden Age for the Greeks and Romans and a similar Age of Truth in Hindu mythology. There is the Garden of Eden for Jews, Christians and Muslims. Tennyson (1842, 1947, pp. 45, 50), following Homer, describes the seductive attraction of the land of the Lotos-Eaters, 'where all things always seemed the same', where 'slumber is more sweet than toil'. Neumann, a younger contemporary of Jung, calls this state of 'slumber' – that is, unconsciousness, or merger with another person or with the universe – 'paradisiacal'. He suggests that myths of Paradise represent individual memories of this early time between mother and baby, when, he says, 'oppositions and tensions do not exist'; 'no opposition between ego–Self and maternal environment is possible . . . the unitary reality of paradise prevails in the early post-natal situation' (Neumann, 1973, p. 14).

A day with any mother and newborn baby will refute these views, and it seems more likely that these developmental theories, in ignoring the difficulties of relationship, are *themselves* another myth of paradise. Common sense parents know that, just as in psychotherapy, disappointments are inevitable right from the beginning. Indeed, the fantasy of one-ness can become dangerous if not given up; if extended also into adulthood one of the pair may die when the other dies or leaves home: the fact of their separateness, forced on them in this way, kills them; one literally cannot exist without the other.

Unconscious identity: an intermittent subjective state

Fordham suggests that it is not a developmental phase but an intermittent state – that the infant has her own 'self' at birth, which can temporarily be experienced as not distinct from the self of another (Fordham, 1985, p. 54). Urban, a contemporary Jungian analyst researching infant development, considers similarly that the experience of 'primary identity' is 'a subjective state felt by one person in relation to and in interaction with another, who can experience that same subjective state in relation to the subject' (Urban, 1998, p. 274). Before the infant can maintain as a steady state the differentiation between one internal content and another, and between self and other (cf. Astor, 1995, p. 61), she may at times experience 'identity' with her mother. Winnicott wrote similarly in 1962: 'the baby retains areas of subjective objects along with other areas in which there is some relating to objectively perceived objects, or "not-me" ("non-I") objects' (Winnicott, 1962, p. 57).

Emergence of the ego – collisions with the environment

It is clear that from birth babies possess a keen mind, an observing, differentiating eye and a listening, differentiating ear. But the establishment of the ego, and a sense of identity (of my self) in differentiation from the environment, is a mighty task for the baby. Birth itself is a huge act of de-integration, of meeting with not-me, with an enforced and total change of environment – from moist to dry, from dark to light, from inside to outside. And in daily living every experience will inevitably bring some sense of this discontinuity between me and not-me. Even in a mainly satisfactory feed, the baby will have had to adjust her mouth to the position of the nipple – and the experience of the 'other' is not only inevitable but essential. Pally shows how the development of the infant's brain is experience-dependent, and how new mental capacities emerge as more parts of the brain come on-line. This clearly relates to what psychologists call 'the development of the ego' (Pally, 2000, pp. 1–15).

Some theorists suggest that the baby learns most during times of stress, such as when hungry (Milrod, 2002, p. 11); others consider that contentment provides the optimum context for the baby quietly to observe, and to differentiate herself from, her environment (Zinkin, 1991, pp. 41f.). Winnicott writes sensitively about the need for the mother to 'disillusion' her baby at a rate the baby can tolerate and of how catastrophic it is if this process does not go well (Winnicott, 1951, pp. 11–15).

According to her instinctual, pre-programmed pattern, the baby puts out 'feelers' towards her environment. The 'feeler' may be crying, looking, touching, rooting for the breast, feeding, excreting or kicking. It is the earliest manifestation of the baby's archetypal, instinctive adaptation to the facts of the world, what Jung calls the 'urge' towards as much conscious psychic wholeness as possible. The baby is looking for a response, and the environment (mother) provides it. Fordham calls this process *de-integration*; it represents an unfolding from the psychosomatic unity of the primary self. Experiences of *re-integrating* the environment's responses lead gradually to the formation of the ego as the baby experiences her agency, and her existence in space and, later, in time (cf. Astor, 1995, pp. 53ff.). In Jung's terminology, these islands of consciousness, arising from the sea of unconsciousness, gradually come together to form the ego; but this ego-island remains always surrounded by the sea, because, 'like the sea itself, the unconscious yields an endless and self-replenishing abundance of living creatures, a wealth beyond our fathoming' (Jung, 1928b, p. 51, 1946, p. 178).

While working as a child psychiatrist, Fordham noticed that children as young as one year old might draw a circle at the same time as using the word 'I' or 'me'. He believed that this was not merely coincidence and considered that this use of 'I' refers to the establishment of an ego separate from a self, that is, to a conscious awareness of the existence of their own self. He notes that it is sometimes impossible with a young child to differentiate the functioning of the self from that of the ego, and that drawing a circle can represent either. He reports other research that shows children using the word 'I' quite regularly at around eighteen months, the presumption then being that they have been using the word for some time (Fordham, 1957, pp. 134, 148–149, 1955, p. 113).

Many cultures may represent this universally repeated dawning of consciousness in myths that extol the creation of light in the original darkness of the world. Christian tradition, Jung suggests, also offers the image of the birth of Jesus as the son of God – 'of the same substance' as the Father (Creed) – to symbolize the ego being 'born' out of the self. Circles and spheres – often the image for a god, or for wholeness/completeness – can also be used to refer to the ego and the self, or to the whole psyche. In the totality of the psyche, 'the conscious mind is contained like a smaller circle within a larger one' (Jung, 1940–1941, p. 258).

Fear of dis-integration

We have to leave the 'Paradise' of unconscious identity, of remaining undifferentiated from both our unconscious psyche and our environment, in order to grow up. And the Bible says that leaving Paradise meant hard work, and suffering, and death (Genesis 3).

Sometimes the disillusionment is too much, and can indeed be deadly. This is sometimes observed when infants 'fail to thrive'. More often, difficulties at this stage do not result in physical illness but in mental illness. What is 'too much' will vary from one baby to another, depending on her innate personality and the experiences she has already had, before or after birth, and in introjecting and identifying with her parents' projections. It will depend partly on her parents' capacity to respond to her de-integrating 'feeler'. For instance, Klein observed that the infant's ability to explore in phantasy her mother's body fosters the wish to explore and learn about all other aspects of life and the world around us. But the mother may block her baby's phantasies if she has a need to protect her own psyche–soma from any kind of penetration. Her baby is then likely to feel that wanting to get inside and explore is too much, is greedy, is damaging; and she may learn not to know about her curiosity and hunger.

If the baby is not able to re-integrate an experience because of its overwhelming intensity, she may feel as if she is dis-integrating – falling to pieces. If dis-integration is to be prevented, the experience may be dissociated, split off and projected. This entails a denial of some aspect of the person's own psyche so that the ego in childhood and still in the adult cannot relate to that aspect of the person's self.

CHAPTER FIVE

EGO DEVELOPMENT IN THERAPY WITH ADULTS

'The biblical fall of man presents the dawn of consciousness
as a curse. And as a matter of fact it is in this light
that we first look upon every problem that
forces us to greater consciousness'
(Jung, 1930, p. 388)

In this chapter, we see how for some adults the unfolding of the self through de-integration, and the gradual enlargement and strengthening of the ego through the process of re-integrating whatever the experience was found to be, has not progressed well enough in childhood. Through clinical examples, we consider different degrees of damage and different types of defence, and how these can be worked with in therapy.

Assessment of ego-strength

We need to try to assess before beginning therapy that the patient's ego is strong enough to sustain what they may experience as assaults upon it – or to know that the therapy will be, at least at first, to strengthen the ego. But since that very strengthening depends on the ego integrating previously unconscious aspects of the psyche, this is a very difficult assessment to make. In therapy, it is always 'as if one were digging an artesian well and ran the risk of stumbling on a volcano' (Jung, 1917, p. 114).

Assessment is not an exact science. Whether a patient has a strong enough ego depends not only on their own resources, but also on the circumstances of the therapy – how much in tune the therapist is, and how well contained the therapist feels, by their own therapy, by supervision, by their experience, by the therapeutic setting, by the theories they work from.

Defences

Meeting a patient for the first time, the therapist will immediately encounter their defensive system. This system will be related to developmental issues and will represent the whole spectrum of psychopathology. Some examples are given below. All defences are intended to protect the patient from unbearable psychic pain; the therapist may also come to understand them as communicating something about the pain they are designed to hide.

Enactment

Harlow, a Jungian analyst specializing in forensic psychiatry, considers some kinds of enactment – crimes such as exhibitionism, shoplifting, and murder – as 'malign individuation'; the behaviour is expressing (albeit in criminal ways) an unknown, denied aspect of the enactor's psyche so that it can be thought about and attended to. Harlow notes that, in all the cases he describes, great changes did occur in the perpetrators' lives, as their unconscious anxieties and longings became available to the consciousness and containment provided by others – through the courts and the National Health Service. The external containment of prison or hospital seemed to be what these people sought, in place of the psychic containment that was not available to them (Harlow, 1996).

As a stage in an ongoing therapy, less severe forms of this kind of enactment are not necessarily malign, if they can be returned to the therapy to be thought about. A patient cutting herself and requiring medical attention, or going on a drunken rampage and spending the night in a police cell, can be thought of as alerting the therapist to particular difficulties that cannot be spoken about, perhaps cannot at that stage be known and so expressed in any other way.

Other people seek external containment for impulses that unconsciously disturb them by identifying with the 'good', or ego-syntonic, aspect of themselves, working in hospitals or schools, the police or the armed forces, in social work or the Samaritans, or by joining religious or psychotherapy organizations.

We can think of such enactments as ways the ego has of defending itself against knowing more of the unconscious psyche – of defending itself against the self. We can also think of them as means the self uses to try to be known – as purposeful messages from the unconscious psyche to the ego, or to another person it hopes will take notice.

Psychosomatic symptoms

It is not always possible to distinguish physical illness from emotional expression. Is the psyche of a person with poor blood circulation and cold hands trying to tell us that she has problems with reaching out and grasping what she wants in the world? Or does she have heart problems that are not related to her emotional 'heart', to her feelings? Or is it both—and, rather than either–or? High blood pressure is often attributed by the medical profession to 'stress' – a catch-all, undefined term. We often find in our work that when the pressure of unspoken, often unthought, feelings is released through words, the patient's blood pressure goes down. Similarly, a patient who cuts herself and watches the blood flow to release what she experiences as intolerable emotional pressure, is likely to need this form of relief less often when she can know her feelings and let them flow, in words, towards her therapist. In both instances, emotional pressure is experienced through the blood.

Psychosomatic illness can protect the ego from potential disintegration, when psychic suffering is expressed and contained in the body as illness rather than in the mind as feelings. Psychosomatic symptoms can intensify as therapy continues. Bad objects previously projected return to the body-psyche, and can be experienced as physically damaging if the patient cannot yet bear to know about them.

Defences of the primary self

In an extreme situation, where psychic death is threatening, the psyche may build what Fordham calls 'defences of the self': a solid wall round the self, impenetrable. The ego does not then develop; egress from, or entry into, this bunkered self is most strictly barred. Redfearn suggests that it makes more sense to think of this 'self', so heavily defended, as 'an early ego', and that Fordham, in private correspondence, agreed with him (Redfearn, 1985, p. 14). (The psychic state is well-evidenced; but the terminology to describe it is, as so often, difficult to pin down.) In this state, the terror of any encounter with not-me is total. For fear of total dis-integration, total breakdown, nothing at all must change. Relations between the patient's ego and their objects are paralysed, and so are relations between the patient's ego and their self. This situation is like that which Kalsched describes as 'archetypal defenses of the personal spirit' (Kalsched, 1996).

Such people may, at particular times, in a particular need, use defences of the self in the consulting room – such as not hearing what the therapist says; or mishearing; or claiming that it makes no sense; or not remembering it; or dismissing it as evidence of the therapist's own need to speak in that way; or devaluing it as useless. At such a time we can think of the patient's self as projected into the therapist; conscious awareness of both must be fended off. This process is symbolized in the Christian story of Herod's massacre of the innocents – he killed all baby boys under two years old: the old ego-regime is terrified of the possibility of a new birth, of change. In such desperate exchanges between patient and therapist, there is often not a clear distinction between a psychic and a somatic defence, or attack. Both therapist and patient may experience their encounter in concretely physical ways: the therapist's countertransference experience is that his words and even his own body are being cut up, or twisted, or fragmented, blocked or deflected, or thrown back. On their side, a patient may put up a hand to protect his head from what is said; or clutch his stomach, where he feels a physical pain as the therapist's remark enters his gut like a dart, or like poison.

Not-dreaming

Not-dreaming (or not remembering dreams) may be a useful and necessary defence against the eruption in near-hallucinatory, terrifying images of contents which the weakened ego could not manage. It is common for patients not to remember dreams until they feel well settled into their therapy. Other patients, of course, hurl themselves into what they trust to be a safe container, and their dreams tumble out from the beginning of the work. But if contents from the unconscious psyche have already overwhelmed the ego, and the person is living in a psychotic, or largely delusional, world, again they may not dream because they are already living in, enacting, their dream world. Images for them are experienced as facts, not symbols (Bion, 1957, p. 51, 1958, p. 78). There is no separate 'dreamer', self-consciously able to observe the activities of other parts of the psyche.

Projection to retain the unity of the psyche

Projection is both an essential means of finding out who we are – we always first encounter new aspects of our selves when they are projected on to others (on to people, objects, ideas) – and also a major defence against know-ing who we are. Jung notes:

> The effect of projection is to isolate the subject from his environment, since instead of a real relationship to it there is now only an illusory one. Projections change the world into the replica of one's own unknown face. In the last analysis, therefore, they lead to an autoerotic or autis-tic condition in which one dreams a world whose reality remains forever unattainable. (Jung, 1951, p. 9)

A patient frequently has a series of illusory relationships with their therapist. We call this the transference. When, for instance, de-integrating feelers hoping for comfort, loving cuddles, loving words, generous feeding, are repeatedly disappointed in the baby, these needs may be denied but projected in adulthood into someone else, such as the therapist. The therapist is then experienced as the needy, hungry, desperate, lonely baby whom the patient, resentfully, feels they have to provide for. Another person might split off and project his rage but identify with the vulnerable, needy aspects of his self: he might then become perhaps permanently ill, or be prone to recurring bouts of illness, or to accidents; or he might create situations in relationships where he was the victim of emotional or physical violence, or where his partner earned the money and ran the household. Such projections or enactments often block vulnerable or unacceptable (shadow) aspects from becoming conscious. As long as he is saying, 'These things happen to me or are done to me', he is projecting his power and so also his responsibility for his own psychic state. These processes are frequently experienced in the therapeutic relationship.

Problematic ego development

There are patients who are not suitable for psychotherapy because their ego is not strong enough. Shakespeare shows us in *King Lear* how, when the old king is deposed (the old ego-defences), other aspects of the psyche are not able to rule the kingdom wisely. Urgent seeking for power, cruelty and ruthlessness, greed and lust, lead in this play to chaos, both in the mind of the old deposed king, who goes mad, and in the civil war that engulfs and destroys the country. The youngest daughter, truth-telling Cordelia, dies. The ego cannot always bear the full truth of psychic reality.

One of the Greek stories also illustrates this dilemma: Theseus and Peirithous go confidently into the Underworld to abduct Persephone. However, they become overwhelmed by the enormity of their undertaking and sit down to rest. They become stuck to the rock and have to be rescued by Heracles. Jung interprets that they have got stuck in their exploration of their unconscious psyches, stuck 'in the wonderland of this inner world', stuck in a longing to stay regressed and not have to cope with daylight and responsibility (Jung, 1952b, p. 293). Should this happen in therapy, the therapist may or may not prove to be a Heracles.

Jung gives a dramatic example of a young man who got caught in this 'wonderland'. He was jilted, and thought of drowning himself, but he 'glimpsed a Dantesque vision' of stars reflected in the river as if they were pairs of divine lovers carried along locked in a dreaming embrace. He wanted to have this immense treasure for himself. As a result, he was arrested trying to break into the nearby astronomical observatory. Jung comments that '[h]e did not drown in the river, but in an eternal image' (Jung, 1928a, p. 146). He could not symbolize; he got stuck in a literal enactment of trying to reach for the stars. His ego was overwhelmed by the archetypal image of being with the woman he loved.

Jung reports a dream from his student days in which he is walking at night, in fog and a mighty wind, with his hands cupped around a tiny light. 'Everything depended on my keeping this little light alive,' he says. Then suddenly he sees behind him a gigantic black figure. On waking, he realizes this is his own shadow on the swirling mists, 'brought into being by the little light I was carrying.' The light, he knows, is his own consciousness –

'[t]hough infinitely small and fragile in comparison with the powers of darkness, it is still a light, my only light' (Jung, 1962, pp. 107f.).

The powers of darkness that could extinguish the light of his consciousness are elements in his unconscious psyche, particularly those he referred to as 'the shadow' – all that our ego does not wish to know that we also are. In therapy, everything depends on the 'little light of consciousness', i.e., the ego, being kept alive. If it is extinguished, serious mental breakdown occurs. There follow some clinical examples, illustrating a gradation from a patient whose ego was overwhelmed to one whose ego was able to integrate a considerable amount of 'shadow'.

Clinical examples

The ego overwhelmed: Elena

Elena was born to an Asian father and an English mother, but had been adopted as a baby by a white English couple. When she herself had a baby, it seemed to activate her feelings of having been abandoned by her birth parents. Her ego was overwhelmed by these previously unconscious feelings of being a desperate, helpless infant – and she became unable to cope with her own baby's needs. There was a risk that she might have suffered a post-natal psychotic breakdown and lost all capacity to function in the ordinary world, but as it was her GP referred her to the local psychiatric unit as suffering from depression. The psychiatrist gave her medication, and offered her therapy, which she attended only grudgingly. The help from the therapist was not enough for her 'abandoned child', and she continued to look for someone to care for her more comprehensively.

She developed a delusion that an Asian man who lived a few doors away down her street was her natural father; she interpreted his neighbourly smiles and greetings as covert messages that he loved her and would care for her. When he did not respond to her meaningful glances, she tested him by purposely upsetting the baby's pushchair so that he could 'rescue' them. But he failed to assist her in any way, and she became very angry with him and threatened to bang on his door demanding answers. The therapist was anxious about the deterioration in her mental state, and it was helpful that Elena was being treated in a hospital setting. This meant that psychiatric referral and intervention were less complicated, and that other members of the team were available for consultation and to provide continuity of care for Elena when the therapist was on holiday. Both therapist and patient were also more adequately contained within the institutional setting, which usually feels more solid and less destructible than a private consulting room.

When the therapist's contract was about to end, but before Elena consciously knew that he would be leaving, she fell in love with a man who lived outside her own town and abruptly moved away. Elena probably knew her therapist would soon be leaving through unconscious communication (see diagram, Chapter Six) and so had left him before he could abandon her. She had also replaced him with someone else she could hope would care for her better.

Mediating the archetype: Francis

Another patient, Francis, also lacked a containing ego, and was consequently at the mercy of various aspects of his unconscious psyche. He, however, was better able to find in the therapist an auxiliary ego he could use to help him function in external reality, until after some time he had internalized it enough to enable him to live a more independent life.

At the beginning of his therapy, he sought for containment in all-protecting clothes, in his armchair, his bed, his house, the consulting room. Time boundaries needed to be very firm, to contain him. He also partially identified with the archetypal image of the saviour – not as in a psychosis where someone thinks they actually have to save the world. His was more the mentality seen in many war and apocalyptic films, where the saviour archetype is enacted: people save their comrades – *Black Hawk Down*, *Saving Private Ryan* – or they save the world from environmental disaster – *The Day After Tomorrow*, *Typhoon* – or from being taken over by aliens – *Independence Day*. With Francis, it took the form of his thinking he would travel to Africa and save a village community by his efforts – though in reality he could not at that time even take a bus to travel from his home to the consulting room; he had to take a taxi, to make him feel safely contained in the dangerous outside world.

He wished to remain as unaware as possible of this outside world. Air on his skin, or rain, or people looking at him in the street, feeling his own sweat, becoming aware of his breathing from physical exertion – all reminded him of 'outside' and were intolerable: hence long trousers, coat, hat, scarf, gloves, dark glasses, a slow pace, not carrying shopping, not waiting for a bus. This fear of being invaded, or damaged, by 'not-me' affected also his relations with his own psyche. He did not risk knowing more differentiated aspects of his own self. He knew nothing of his rage, disappointment, envy, longing for love. The Christian symbol for this state is God before the birth of Jesus – a unity. When the Son is born, that is, our ego develops, Satan also comes into being – we become aware of our own shadow. Satan's alternative name is Lucifer, the bringer of light; and Francis could not bear to have his unconscious psyche brought into the light of consciousness. He could experience himself only as gentle, caring and altruistic. He imagined himself as an idolized, immensely wealthy pop-star, desired by innumerable beautiful women and giving large sums of money to the poor; any life-style less than this would not do. So he could not attempt anything mundane, could not learn and make mistakes. He had to stay in a state of primary, or original, unity – God-like, baby-like, but certainly unde-integrated. Usually his therapist experienced him as more like an infant; but occasionally his arrogance, his annihilation of time, therapist, money, all reality, took his therapist's breath away, and her private associations then were to a God who destroyed the whole world because it displeased him.

Francis feared that the end of the world was imminent and that he would be destroyed (for instance, he stock-piled cans of food in advance and was terrified through-out the night of the end of the last century). This was a projection of his own (Satanic) wish to annihilate the world that was 'not me' and therefore not under his control. He had no internal space in which he could store his experience of his therapist – so he kept all her bills, to reassure him that the sessions had actually taken place. He also hoarded all sorts of items – newspapers, letters, yoghurt pots, furniture – in case he needed them; so his flat was crowded. He intended to donate the yoghurt pots to a local children's playgroup (the 'saviour' fantasy).

His therapist's task was to help Francis symbolize and develop his own ego to create a space for self-reflection and where he could store his internal good objects. Another way of thinking about this work is that the therapist was mediating, that is, humanizing, Francis's archetypal experience. In place of the fantasies of being a saviour to remote people, or even to local toddlers, Francis experienced that his therapist was 'saving' him in very unremarkable ways – helping him to get up in the morning to get to his sessions, helping him to manage his money by insisting he pay his fees. So Francis learned that the 'saviour' image could usefully be enacted in everyday matters, and that he could 'save' his own self. Similarly, his archetypal (projected) rage of world-destruction became somewhat integrated into his ego as a moderate, ordinary rage that his therapist was outside his control, in the timing of the sessions, and in her going away on breaks. In this way, modest amounts at a time of what had been unthought-about aspects of his unconscious psyche were integrated into his ego. As some of his own rage became ego-syntonic, less was projected, and so the external world seemed less dangerous. In the same process, his ego was enlarged and his anxiety became less; and so he became more able to contain it.

Any unmediated archetype can destroy the ego: we read in Greek stories that, when Zeus showed himself to her, Semele was burned up with his radiance. We read also that the look of Medusa turned a person to stone; but

Perseus looked at her safely when she was reflected in his shield, and so he was able to kill her. The therapist's mind acts as the reflecting shield, in which the patient can safely see his archetypal images, and so can bear them.

After a few years, Francis became able to throw away some of his hoard. He became able to travel to his sessions by bus. He arrived on time. He joined his local church, and got to church on time, and to some evening meetings. He had a succession of short-lived part-time jobs. He was able to attend some evening classes – though he did not complete a course. In summer, he could wear lighter clothing, though he still needed long sleeves.

Ego development: Greta

Greta's ego was less severely impaired than Francis's was. She was married, had two teenage children and a part-time job. She kept an eye on her widowed mother, who lived in the next street and had a long psychiatric history. But Greta had little sense of her own continuity over time. She was in therapy for two years, at the start of which she said her mind was like a can of spaghetti, all tangled up. She needed to develop an ego-capacity to relate to the external reality of her own history – and so to the experience of having a self which existed steadily through time. She spent two years putting her memories in order – going over and over the sequence in time of when her parents had moved, when her mother had gone into hospital, when a younger brother had been born, when she had changed schools, when she had played with different groups and gangs of children, when she had fallen off a wall, when she had had her hair cut – and on into her early adult life, where there was still no smooth, comprehensible sequence of events: when she had had her first boyfriend, started her first job, met her husband. This steady work turned her can of worms into a spaghetti junction: her ego could think about her self.

This was achieved through her ability to internalize her therapist's capacity to think about her chaotic experiences and to make sense of them – to hold them in his mind without being overwhelmed by them. Her therapist enacted the good mother who can bear her child in mind even when the child is physically absent. This Greta's mother had not been able to do – when Greta went out to play, her mother had no concern for her; Greta remembered walking along a railway bridge parapet, and her mother never knowing about it. The therapist provided structure and regularity, in the security of the framework of the therapy, and Greta was able to internalize this experience. As a result, she became less depressed, and was able to think about her external life in the present; she made several changes: she arranged for her mother to go into a nursing home; she went on a training course and got a better job; she and her husband enjoyed a holiday together.

But Greta did not risk this new-found stability by trying to integrate more of her unconscious psyche into her ego. She was resistant to thinking about her therapist in any other than an idealized light – as compensation for the inadequacies she had suffered from her mother. That her therapist might also be in some ways inadequate, or annoying, was intolerable. So she left the therapy, having achieved at age forty the adequately functioning ego which more fortunate people develop in childhood. Her therapist did not try to persuade her to stay. He remembered Jung writing:

71

I am inclined to take deep-seated resistances seriously at first, paradoxical as this may sound, for I am convinced that the doctor does not necessarily know better than the patient's own psychic constitution, of which the patient himself may be quite unconscious. (Jung, 1929a, pp. 39f.)

Integrating the shadow: Harriet

Harriet was highly defended against knowing anything about her unconscious psyche, particularly about her longing to be cared for and her need to dominate other people so that they would not leave her, both of which she projected into many other people and situations – for instance, she was a care-worker in a residential home. The experience of two-ness, of difference, gave her extreme dis-ease. So she had a do-it-yourself approach to therapy, constantly talking about not needing to come. Yet, she also complained that her therapist kept her at a distance; she wanted to stay either omnipotently alone or in a regressed, 'merged' state. In any dispute at work, she assured her therapist that everyone in the team agreed with her; she needed to maintain a delusional uniformity between herself and them. This is a common need, imaged in the Christian view of Heaven, where the choir of angels sing and dance in harmony, where God is 'one', and the persons of the Trinity, all 'of one substance', are in harmonious (self-)communication. Only when others 'mirrored' her, by being the same as she, could Harriet feel that her existence was tolerable to them and therefore to her. When her therapist did not see things her way, he became to her like the unharmonious Satan, the chaotic lawless power who disrupted the peace of Heaven, and she wished to leave the therapy as a way of expelling this 'Satan' from her 'Heaven'. At such times, her therapist broke the mirror, and Harriet then felt as if her whole psyche had been viciously attacked and lay shattered in pieces. She gradually came to be aware of a desperate loneliness, created by her monolithic obliteration of the individuality and separateness of other people.

She obliterated similarly any awareness of her own shadow – dissenting voices within her own psyche – so that she could experience herself as a unity, as a totally conscientious, friendly person, and her line-manager as unreasonable, ungrateful, manipulative, and selfish. She experienced her therapist also like this. But because it was possible to work on the details of her perception of her therapist, Harriet gradually came to realize that it was *she* who forgot her cheque, *she* who refused to talk, *she* who would not listen to any disagreement, *she* who hated him. As Jung writes in 'The psychology of the transference',

> The individual's specious unity that emphatically says '*I* want, *I* think' breaks down under the impact of the unconscious. So long as the patient can think that somebody else (his father or mother) is responsible for his difficulties, he can save some semblance of unity (*putatur unus esse!*). But once he realizes that he himself has a shadow, that his enemy is in his own heart, then the conflict begins and one becomes two.' (Jung, 1946, p. 198; original italics)

Harriet became aware of the conflict in her own heart between wanting to push her therapist away and wanting to get closer to him. So then she had to try to know what it was that 'she' more fully wanted. Harriet came to know that she was not this fictitious, totally friendly, co-operative

73

person; she was in fact a complicated mixture of co-operation and rebellion, of caring for others and wanting herself to be cared for.

Towards individuation

Jung writes: 'Individuation is an exceedingly difficult task: it always involves a conflict of duties, whose solution requires us to understand that our "counter-will" is also an aspect of God's will' (Jung, 1942, p. 198); that is, it is also an aspect of our total psyche. And to live with this knowledge Jung compares to Jesus telling his disciples to take up their cross and follow him – we become '[n]o longer a mere selection of suitable fictions, but a string of hard facts, which together make up the cross we all have to carry or the fate we ourselves are' (Jung, 1946, p. 199). Carrying this cross means we are uncertain about ourselves, because we know we are not a simple unity. Jung tells of a patient's dream, in which the white magician is dressed in black and the black magician is dressed in white. Each needs the wisdom of the other (Jung, 1928a, p. 182).

CHAPTER SIX

THE SELF–EGO RELATIONSHIP IN THE THERAPIST

'The doctor is as much "in the analysis" as the patient'
(Jung, 1929b, p. 72)

Figure 1 is an adaptation of a diagram Jung devised to illustrate the phenomenon of the transference (Jung, 1946, p. 221).

To consider first the in*tra*psychic dynamics illustrated here: Fordham added the line (D) to show that the patient blocks, through defence mechanisms, unconscious material from becoming conscious (Fordham, 1978, p. 87). The therapist is shown as having no such block. This is an idealistic portrayal of the totally conscious therapist – obviously an impossibility. Their own therapy, however, is

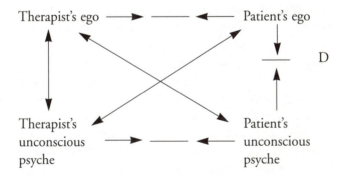

Figure 1. The phenomenon of the transference. Source: Fordham, 1978, p. 87

intended to make the therapist less defensive than the patient against messages from their own unconscious psyche.

The diagram also shows the complex int*er*psychic communications between therapist and patient: from ego to ego, from ego to unconscious, from unconscious to ego, and from unconscious to unconscious, in both directions.

Countertransference: sorting out whose feeling is whose

The therapist's task is to distinguish her affect from her patient's, and so to find her own reality as distinct from her patient's – and to distinguish her feelings towards her patient from her feelings towards other people. Only then can she help her patient disentangle his projections and own his own feelings. For example: when a patient was planning her wedding in the same month as the therapist's daughter of about the same age, it was understandably difficult for the therapist to separate her feelings about her own daughter's marriage from those about her patient's marriage. Sometimes she became caught up in her identification of her daughter with her patient: *who* was planning to wear a red wedding-dress?

Another therapist realized how fed-up he was feeling with a particular patient. He worked hard in supervision to understand why his patient was needing to make him feel like that – and in his own therapy to understand his own reasons for feeling impatient with her. Understanding his own feelings in these ways renewed his interest in his work with this patient. In the next session, she said that he looked fed-up with her. Having prepared himself he found that, without either confirming or contradicting her impression, he could with some confidence suggest that perhaps *she* felt fed-up with *him* (because he had misunderstood something she had said in the previous session). She immediately acknowledged that she was not best pleased about this, thought it had wasted her time, and was anxious in case it happened again in this session. So his work on his countertransference had, in a small way, assisted his patient in acknowledging her own feelings and no longer attributing them to her therapist.

It is not always so straightforward. At another time, this therapist was feeling less secure in himself than usual – his marriage was going through a rocky period and so he was feeling less secure in his work. In one session, he felt great fear, and the image of a deer being torn to pieces by hounds came into his mind. He wondered whether this was his patient's fear, that he would savagely attack anything she said to him; or whether it was his own fear that in his more precarious emotional state he would not work well and that his colleagues would tear him to pieces for his incompetence. He remembered the fear he had felt at being criticized by his Maths teacher for not doing his homework properly, when he had not properly understood it. He remembered also the story of Adonis, killed by a boar after he had repulsed Venus's advances: was it his fear that his patient would attack him for repulsing her (as yet unconscious) erotic feelings? He could not tell where the true location of this feeling of fear was, at that moment in the session. So, bearing all this in mind, he waited to see how the situation might evolve. He did not relieve himself of his anxiety by assuming that it was not his fear, in case he might be evacuating his feelings into his patient, and thus doing the reverse of what the therapy should be doing: helping each person to recognize and own their own self.

The therapist's assumptions

Therapists need to be aware not only of personal but also of collective denial: groups or whole societies can project unwanted aspects of their unconscious psyches on to other groups. We may want to respond to the collective and political dimension, as well as to the personal, when a patient brings us experiences of, for instance, racial abuse, whether as perpetrator or recipient. And there are some situations – such as child abuse or the imminence of violence – when it is a therapist's ethical responsibility to take action. We are legally obliged to bow to the collective.

The therapist is operating within society and often needs to be aware of those delicate ethical moments when social responsibility seems to (or does) transcend the claims of intrapsychic development. With these issues it is very difficult (or some would say unethical) to suspend judgement. A patient wants to kill themselves; we understand the rage and despair, perhaps the desire for revenge, but do we 'know' that for this patient, at this time, suicide would be wrong? We are not simply neutral facilitators of our patient's psychic process: we affect it. We have to hold the impossible position of knowing that we have some responsibility for the effect our work has on our patient and their family, yet also knowing that we cannot know what would be better or possible for that person at that time.

Theoretical assumptions, which may at the time seem to be absolute, sometimes turn out later to have been only relatively true. For example, with Freud and Jung and their immediate successors, the usual pattern was male therapist and female patient, and the reality of the impact of the therapist's gender was accepted without question. The assumption was that a male therapist would evoke the transference to father. Similarly, with the arrival of female therapists such as Klein, it was assumed that to them the predominant transference would be to mother. Today, all theorists consider that both male and female therapists can be experienced in the transference as 'mother' and as 'father'. The therapist is always 'other' to the patient, and so is able to receive the projection of the patient's unconscious psyche, which is 'other' to their ego.

Our identity, out of which we speak to our patients, is affected by theoretical, clinical, personal, and cultural assumptions. The therapist may aim to be a 'blank screen', so that it would make little difference who they are, whether they are man or woman. Yet clearly these things do make a difference to the patient and to the course of the therapy. And if the therapist is 'in' the therapy along with the patient – if both sit in chairs, and make eye contact and relate to each other as particular people – then the personality and sex of the therapist can be acknowledged and worked with rather than its impact being denied.

Some non-psychodynamic therapists think it is their job to decide for the patient what the patient wants, or should want. Some Christian counsellors assume, for instance, that homosexuality is a spiritual and moral wrong, and that it is their task to try to change a patient's sexual orientation to heterosexual. And even with the best intentions to be unbiased, it is impossible for any therapist not to have unconscious prejudices that will

inevitably infect the work. Many psychodynamic therapists, for instance, impose collective norms, such as that
to be in a relationship is 'better', a sign of greater
emotional health, than to be single.

Jung made some ringing statements about respecting
individual life-choices – '[t]he shoe that fits one person
pinches another; there is no universal recipe for living'.
His concept of individuation is exactly as variable as the
differences between people, because it is based on the
premise that '[e]ach of us carries his own life-form within
him – an irrational form which no other can outbid'
(Jung, 1929a, p. 41).

Bion and Fordham are both in the same theoretical
position as Jung. Bion states that we should suspend
'memory and desire' in order to free the psyche of the
therapist from assumptions (Bion, 1970, p. 82). Fordham
writes about 'not knowing beforehand', of locking up our
filing cabinet of memory and theory, so that we are free
to respond to this person at this moment (Fordham,
1993). The ideal as he sees it is that we don't know what
is going to happen, we don't know what is best for our
patient; only their own psyche knows; it is our job to
listen, and to follow, not in any sense to lead.

Our patients always bring to therapy from the beginning their own potential for greater wholeness, health and
growth. As well as being the source of their own misery,
they are also always the source of their own healing. As
Winnicott says, 'The principle is that it is the patient and
only the patient who has the answers' (Winnicott, 1969,
p. 102). The therapist's job is to act as midwife to the
birth of their self. Jung writes:

> Individuation appears, on the one hand, as the synthesis
> of a new unity which previously consisted of scattered

particles, and on the other hand, as the revelation of something which existed before the ego and is in fact its father or creator and also its totality. (Jung, 1940–1941, p. 263)

Working with projections of the self archetype

It can be difficult for a therapist to distinguish the reality of who she is when parts of her can identify with a patient's projections, and when she is experienced so differently, and so intensely, at different times. This can become particularly difficult when the transference projections have an archetypal dimension, when a patient actually perceives her therapist's face as stony, inflamed with anger, deathly pale, or bored beyond endurance – or, occasionally, as transformed with a light of beauty. The therapist receives projections of the patient's self, both in its many part-aspects and also in its fullness.

The 'idealizing' transference–countertransference

This idealizing transference may result from the patient wanting to experience the therapist as a totally loving mother in compensation for her own internal neglectful or cruel mother – she projects on to the therapist the opposite pole of the archetype. But it is also created by her projection of her own wonderful self, full of light and creative potential. It is important that the therapist does not identify with either of these projections. The dangers are inflation and acting out.

If the therapist identifies with an internal image of someone who is 'healed', then they are projecting their own 'sick' aspects on to the patient, instead of acknowledging

81

that they are, at best, a 'wounded healer' (Guggenbuhl-Craig, 1971, pp. 85–101; cf. Jung, 1940–1941, p. 293). Patients may, of course, unconsciously encourage this splitting, as it leaves the therapist with the power and the responsibility, and the patient can then also imagine that *someone* understands and is in control of psychic processes.

The temptation to this identification will be stronger if the therapist is feeling at that time less confident about her capacities, such as when she is in training or when there is stress in her own life. Then to feel centred, balanced, all-encompassing, all-understanding – 'wise and wonderful' – will compensate for her feeling of inferiority. This compensation can also lead to acting-out, as, for instance, by setting a low fee, which can keep the therapist in the role of the totally self-sufficient, all-giving mother, and the patient in an infantile, cared-for state of over-dependence.

The 'erotic' transference–countertransference: reductive and synthetic modes of interpretation

As with the erotic aspects of the relationship between child and parent, the erotic transference–countertransference can be useful in creating strong bonds of affection between patient and therapist. These can, of course, be part of the present reality between the two adults, but we limit our patient's development if we do not understand also its current symbolic meaning. In therapy, these feelings can relate to very early enjoyable and exciting physical contact between a baby and her mother, or to Oedipal longings more directly related to sexual phantasies. But even such developmental and realistic explanations of transference–countertransference eroticism are insufficient on their own.

We therefore need to have available two approaches to interpretation: one is a 'reductive', developmental approach – where we 'reduce' the present material to the original historical situation we think it is revealing; the other is a 'synthetic' approach, where we understand the present material as a communication about what the patient's psyche wants for its future – it wants a 'synthesis' of the unconscious psyche and consciousness, so that the patient will experience more of his self now. A 'synthetic' approach may use a 'reductive' interpretation, as a means of amplifying (that is, turning up the volume, making more distinct) the current internal situation. Both approaches are symbolic; one looks back, the other forward. Most therapists use both, though most put more emphasis on one than the other.

Freud, for instance, favoured the reductive approach, Jung the synthetic. For Jung, 'Incest symbolizes union with one's own being, it means individuation or becoming a self' (Jung, 1946, p. 218). He writes: 'The regressive tendency only means that the patient is seeking *himself* in his childhood memories' (Jung, 1929a, p. 33; original italics). There are here multiple meanings in the word '*himself*'. Jung is suggesting that the patient's regression is to retrieve his experience of himself as a child, even to the experience of a 'primitive identity' with mother/therapist. It is also to return to the original psychosomatic unity of infancy, to regress back to the primary self. Incestuous libido from the mother/therapist equally can result from an identification with the desire of the unconscious psyche of the patient, projected on to the therapist, to become conscious in uniting with the ego (Jung, 1952b,

p. 294). Synthetically, this regression symbolizes the longing to unite consciousness with unconsciousness, the ego with the self, as was the psychic state in infancy.

Reductive and synthetic interpretations: Irene

Irene had been beaten by her father, and, when her father was away, her mother had encouraged her to sleep in the marital bed, until her mid-teens. Her experiences with her father showed in the transference–countertransference relationship as Irene's combined fear and excitement that her therapist would treat her harshly, and in her repeated experience that any interpretation was a blow to her, or had penetrated her both physically and emotionally. But if she found her therapist's tone of voice gentle, or saw a kind look on his face, this also frightened her as she experienced it as seductive, with overtones of her experience with her mother.

The erotic element in the therapeutic relationship was powerful and complicated. For Irene, it was not an incestuous longing, but an incestuous fear – a fear of the only physical relationship she had had with either parent, and an inability to imagine a loving sexual relationship. But her therapist also interpreted Irene's feelings synthetically – that is, he spoke of Irene's expectation that a greater understanding of her self was certain to be painful, difficult, and suffocating – that it would pull her back to an infantile dependence on the therapist (as if in bed with mother) rather than helping her towards a more separate and fulfilled life.

CHAPTER SEVEN

INDIVIDUATION: DIALOGUE WITH ONE'S SELF

'One should cultivate the art of conversation with oneself'
(Jung, 1928a, p. 202)

The Copernican revolution

In the sixteenth century, when the astronomer Copernicus calculated that the earth was not the centre round which all the planets orbited, people had to rethink their view of themselves, God, and the meaning and importance of their lives. The whole of creation was *not* there to serve its crowning glory, humankind.

Freud referred to this event, along with the discoveries of Darwin, to illustrate how people experience as a major blow to their self-love the realization of the power and effects of the unconscious (Freud, 1916–1917, pp. 284f.). Jung also used this event as an image for the psychic revolution that occurs when the ego realizes that it is not the centre of the psyche. Jung acknowledged the shock to the ego, but typically found purpose and hope in this psychic shift – because he emphasized that there is a new centre, the self, around which the ego revolves as the earth revolves round the sun (Jung, 1929a, p. 49). As Jung said: 'The hammer cannot discover within itself the power which makes it strike. It is something outside, something autonomous, which seizes and moves him'

(Jung, 1940–1941, p. 250). This revolution results in a major shift in the personality, not lightly accommodated. Although this submission can become psychotic, entailing the loss of the ego, in health it is a conscious putting of the ego in a subordinate position. Some patients, even from the beginning of their therapy, know they are in the grip of a power beyond their ego-control, the 'self', and they are willing to submit to this power to rethink the meaning and purpose of their lives. Jung's focus on submission to the 'self' is parallel to the notion of submission to God. For example, 'Muslim' means one who has willed total surrender to God. The religious believer speaks of God's grace, of God seeking for the lost soul; the psychologist sees these beliefs as symbols for the start of a stage in the process of individuation.

Grimm's fairy tale, 'The Three Feathers', similarly shows how only from the depths of the unconscious psyche come the riches the ego needs. Here, the king has three sons. In order to determine who should succeed him, he sets them on a quest for valuable objects: a carpet, a jewel, and a woman. He tosses three feathers in the air, and the three sons each follow one of them. The two elder sons range widely on the surface of the land, but the third son observes that one feather has fallen to the ground by his feet. Beside it he sees a trapdoor, and descends into the earth. Below is a frog-queen, who gives him the most elaborate carpet, the most valuable jewel and eventually the most beautiful maiden. The youngest son therefore proves most worthy to inherit his father's kingdom (von Franz, 1970).

Sign, image, symbol

A symbol is 'the best possible expression for a complex fact not yet clearly apprehended by consciousness' (Jung, 1957, p. 75). In this, it is different from a sign, which points towards something already known, such as red meaning 'stop' on a traffic light. It also differs from an image, which is a psychic representation to which meaning has not yet been attributed.

So, for example, a patient may bring at the beginning of a session one particular experience, perhaps a comment about the difficulty of finding somewhere to park the car. From the patient's point of view, this is only a fact, but within the context of the session it can be thought of as an image and hence potentially as a symbol. Individual meaning is carried in the detail, in the context, in the emotional tone. Each symbol is specific – to that person, at that time, in that situation, with that history and those hopes. It is also specific to that moment in the story of the therapy and in the developing relationship between patient and therapist.

The opening conversational gambit of the self – the production of an image or a symptom – is transformed through dialogue with the ego into a symbol. In therapy, the transformation from the literal to the symbolic usually takes place first in the mind of the therapist. The symbol is then available for further consideration by the ego of both therapist and patient.

Symbol out of image: Jason

In his first session, Jason reported three dreams that had haunted him for twenty years – he was then about forty. One was of the illness and death of his father and brother; one was of a mouthful of broken teeth; one was of his desperate searching for a girl he had gone out with briefly in his teens. These traumatic images had to be repeated compulsively because Jason had no means of thinking about them. But he and the therapist came to understand together that these dreams were trying to communicate important psychic facts in a symbolic form – that Jason's internal father and brother had to die, so that he was no longer so dominated by them; that he needed to find his capacity to bite – his aggression, his wish to engage with the world; and that he wanted to find a capacity for head-long, instinctual letting-go, like his teenage falling in love. His self had been trying to get these messages understood for twenty years: 'the ego cannot voluntarily fabricate dreams, but simply dreams what it has to,' writes Jung (1943 pp. 246f.). Within weeks of starting therapy, Jason ceased to dream the first two dreams, and after a couple of years, when the therapeutic pair had more fully engaged with the meaning of the third dream, he also no longer dreamed this. 'Message received. Over and out.'

Symbol out of symptom: Karen

Somatic symptoms can be understood as embodied images. Karen, for instance, over many years before she came to therapy, had severe bowel problems; these were treated medically. Once in therapy she dreamed repeatedly of searching for a lavatory – but none was suitable: they were always dirty, or locked, or occupied, or broken, or inaccessible up a flight of stairs (the consulting room was upstairs). The somatic symptom had developed into a dream image; and Karen was enacting its symbolic mean-ing in the therapy, in discharging into the consulting room/her therapist's mind some of her blocked up feelings: such as her desperate search to find a safe place where she could relieve her psyche of a lifetime of 'bad' feelings.

The therapist gave to Karen an understanding of the symbolic meaning of her physical symptoms and of her dream images, by interpreting in the transference, 'You're telling me that you feel I don't have room in my mind for your feelings' and 'You feel I don't want to know what you suffer'. At another time she interpreted using more body-based language, referring to Karen's 'shitty feelings', and her fear that she would damage the therapist with her shit-bombs. The therapist also related these images to Karen's angry feelings against both her parents, and the impossibility of expressing them when she was a child.

After about six months, Karen's frenetic dreams ceased, and some time later her bowel problems also improved, though they did not go away completely. The message from her self had been understood and translated by her therapist's ego, and that understanding passed to Karen's ego.

Emergence of unifying symbol: Linda

For a long time, Linda was stuck with two images of herself. One was a plastic pot-plant with artificially regular shape. Linda hated this plant – it wasn't real, she said, and it did not grow. She also had the image of a wild and straggly bush, dying for lack of nourishment. Then Linda had a dream. She dreamed of clouds blowing wildly across the sky in the shape of the word 'transformation'. As she woke, she realized that the term 'plastic' could mean flexible, changeable, as clouds can change their shape; it didn't have to mean artificial and sterile. Equally, wild and straggly did not have to mean neglected. Her 'opposite' images, and all they stood for, were ready to be transformed into a new symbol.

The symbol is the 'child' of the coming together of ego and self

Imagery of sexual intercourse between a man and a woman can, of course, have many meanings, relating to the patient's historical past, their external present life or the transference relationship. However, such an image may also symbolize the union of the ego and the unconscious psyche, with the resultant birth of a baby-self. This baby-self is the symbol. An interpretation might include the value for the patient of being able to imagine parental intercourse without needing to destroy it through envy, jealousy, or fear, and so being able to imagine her own internal parents coming together to allow her own creativity to develop, in whatever form was at that time relevant.

Discovering symbols of the self

The child

Confusingly, not only can the symbol be thought of as a 'child', but also 'child' can be a symbol. Psychic development is frequently presented in therapy as an image of a baby being born. Because the primary psychosomatic self, with its full undeveloped potential, occurs at the beginning of our life, the child can always potentially symbolize either the beginning or the goal of the individuation process – both the achievement of one stage and the beginning of the next. Material about a baby being neglected – dropped, not fed properly, suffocated, or passed to someone else to look after – may all be symbols of the particular difficulties the patient is having in looking after her new and fragile self. It is important to be aware that these images may also be referring to a historical, developmental event in the patient's life.

In the Christian tradition, the story that Jesus was conceived by the Virgin Mary of the Holy Spirit symbolizes that the birth-image refers to an internal process rather than being the result of an external union. (Chapters Four and Eight consider the vital supporting role of relationships.)

Abstract or gendered?

Our self is, in its essence, not fully knowable, and any image we have of it is bound to be partial, limited by our personal experience and by the historical and cultural framework within which we live. Any object can give us a glimpse of it – a field of ripe corn, Keats's nightingale, the experience of looking at the stars or of listening to a late Beethoven quartet.

All these are impersonal, non-gendered images. Jung refers to 'the neutral self, the objective fact of totality' as distinct from the personal ego. The self is 'quid', not 'quis' (an object, not a person) (Jung, 1951, p. 164). As the culmination of the first part of one person's individuation process, Jung presents a patient's dream of 'the world clock', a three-dimensional model, in which three interconnected circles pulse and turn rhythmically in relation to each other. This vision brought the dreamer 'the impression of "the most sublime harmony"' (Jung, 1944, pp. 203f.). The impersonal and the abstract are, for Jung, adequate symbols of the self.

In this abstraction, he fails to address an important part of the realization of both the ego and the self. It is a paradox that the self is not personal, yet we can only ever know it through personal (and therefore gendered) experience, or through images that have a personal (and therefore a gendered) meaning. 'Objective' the self may be, but it is also the psychic expression of our autonomous bodily functions, which include functions related to our sexuality. Moreover, it can only be realized in the ego of a person who has become conscious of their sex and gender in their own particular way. Our experience of our self, in our sexed and gendered consciousness, is therefore also necessarily sexed and gendered.

In religious story

Hindu story has a pantheon of gods of both sexes (see Chapter Three), which can helpfully act as symbols of the self for different people at different stages of their psychic development. The Judaic, Christian, and Islamic God, however, is solely masculine. This leaves a deficit, for both men and women, of how to imagine, through their religious imagery, the feminine and the female aspects of their being. The adoration of the Virgin Mary in some branches of the Christian religion goes some way to filling this gap; but our Western patriarchal society, founded on patriarchal religions, does not facilitate the appropriate honouring of being a woman. Christianity, too, often encourages splitting between Mary – bodiless, sexless, obedient, passive, and worshipped – and Eve – rebellious, curious, sexual, in league with the serpent/Satan. This can hamper the integration of a woman's sexuality and assertiveness into an ego-friendly experience.

Since consciousness and the unconscious psyche do affect each other, '[t]he unconscious God-image can therefore alter the state of consciousness, just as the latter can modify the God-image once it has become conscious' (Jung, 1951, p. 194). For psychic health, women and men need a more satisfying image of woman as divine. Princess Diana will not do (cf. Clark, 2003).

The technique of 'active imagination'

Active imagination is a technique that promotes dialogue between the ego and the self. The ego is deliberately set aside temporarily, and images from the unconscious arise and develop; the ego watches the story unfold as in a theatre, noting plot, characters, setting, dialogue. It is important that the unconscious psyche expresses itself as fully as possible, before the ego intervenes to try to understand or interpret. The value of these activities is contained in the value attributed by the ego to the images released from the self. By listening to a patient for a long time in a session and making only later and few interventions, a therapist can facilitate the patient's flow of unconscious material and allow the fantasies to develop.

Active imagination can also be practised without another person. If the patient is on their own, it is obviously important that their ego is able to cope with whatever images and affects the self produces – in a session, the therapist can use their own ego to assist with this. Otherwise, the practitioner of active imagination can be overwhelmed by the emerging unconscious material, and may identify with a sub-personality or feel their ego helpless before the power of a terrifying or beatific image.

Art therapy and drama therapy are based on the theory of active imagination; images can also be formulated in pottery, or poetry. These receptive media are all able to take the practitioner's projections from their self, so that the ego can become aware of them and think about them. As the Buddhist master said when his pupil complained of disconcerting images when he was meditating in front of a white wall, 'Well, the wall isn't doing anything.'

The dialogue is lifelong

At various stages of our adult life, we may experience a terrible sense of futility or rage, when all that has been achieved so far seems inadequate or wrong. At marriage, or ten or so years later when children have been born (or not) and the relationship is as it is, when one career has been chosen and other choices foreclosed, or later when children leave home, we retire from work and enter the 'Third Age' (Hubback, 1996, p. 3) – at any of these stages we may need to face more deeply that our reality does not live up to our ideal longings.

In Indian and Chinese religious traditions, men have often left their homes to spend their last years as beggars or hermits, devoting themselves to introspection or to worship. In Christian mediaeval tradition, it was common for husband and wife to separate into monastery and convent after their children were married – after they had achieved what Freud calls the tasks of young adult life, to love and to work. Their ego-tasks done (adapting to external reality, raising the next generation), they submitted to the will of God. This change in psychic balance is also presented as a sudden shock, as in the story of Saul of Tarsus: his stoning of Stephen, an early disciple of Jesus, led to his traumatic encounter with the risen Christ on the road to Damascus, and his conversion from 'Saul', the persecutor of Jesus's followers, to 'Paul', the preacher of the 'good news' that Jesus was the son of God. Such dramatic conversions are often seen in counsellors and psychotherapists in the early stages of their training: the theories of depth psychology and their experience in therapy make startling, dramatic sense to them, and they talk to everyone in psycho-speak, enthusiastically analysing every situation and evangelizing friends and family.

The dialogue between our ego and our self is a never-completed process. We face daily the ever-renewing abundance of our unconscious psyche and new situations in the external world, with all the complications and feelings these arouse. We can either be dragged along by archetypal forces or, by co-operating with them, harness their power for growth. The goal of individuation, Jung says, 'is important only as an idea; the essential thing is the *opus* which leads to the goal: *that* is the goal of a lifetime' (Jung, 1946, p. 200; original italics).

CHAPTER EIGHT

INDIVIDUATION: RELATING TO OTHER PEOPLE

'We meet ourselves time and again in a
thousand disguises on the path of life'
(Jung, 1946, p. 318)

Self-knowledge and relationships

Jung has often been accused that his 'myth' of individuation is too introspective, insufficiently related to other people or to the needs of society. It is certainly true that his emphasis is more on our inner development. But, as we have seen repeatedly in the clinical illustrations throughout this book, a change in someone's internal world leads inevitably to changes in their external circumstances. In Jung's words:

> relationship to the self is at once relationship to our fellow man, and no one can be related to the latter until he is related to himself . . . Individuation has two principal aspects: in the first place it is an internal and subjective process of integration, and in the second it is an equally indispensable process of objective relationship. Neither can exist without the other. (Jung, 1946, p. 234)

He is saying that as we withdraw the psychic contents we have projected onto our neighbour, we simultaneously both acknowledge these feelings as our own and also thereby see our neighbour more accurately as himself.

In all the areas in which therapist or patient is not fully self conscious, they are linked to the other person only through projections. Winnicott (1969) describes movingly and clearly how a baby can move from 'relating' to a person to 'using' that person – though his terminology is the reverse of that more usually employed. For Winnicott, 'relating' means what Jung in the following passage refers to as 'primitive identity with others', and Winnicott's 'using' is what Jung and others call 'relationship'. Winnicott is writing about a baby and his mother, Jung about adults; but the difference they are describing is the same – the difference between the subject's not-knowing and knowing the separateness and distinction between himself and the other.

Jung writes of the difficulty in making this transition:

> In order to be conscious of myself, I must be able to distinguish myself from others. Relationship can only take place where this distinction exists. But although the distinction may be made in a general way, normally it is incomplete, because large areas of psychic life still remain unconscious. As no distinction can be made with regard to unconscious contents, on this terrain no relationship can be established; here there still reigns the original unconscious condition of the ego's primitive identity with others, in other words a complete absence of relationship . . .Unconsciousness results in non-differentiation, or unconscious identity. The practical consequence of this is that one person presupposes in the other a psychological structure similar to his own. (Jung, 1925, pp. 190, 192)

We live, then, for much of the time, seeing in other people not their real selves but a replica of our own unknown face, and experiencing our own self as less than we fully are. We are divided, with part of our self in us and part projected into the other. As we differentiate ourselves from others, we become more undivided, more of an 'individual', And since projections are always unconscious, for each projected feeling acknowledged, a tiny piece more of our unconscious psyche has become conscious. The work of individuation has moved forward. The formality and reliability of the therapeutic relationship – though not of that relationship exclusively – facilitate this movement.

Morality: collective or individual?

Individuation involves learning to live in the real world. Jung writes further that a widening of consciousness 'is a function of relationship to the world of objects, bringing the individual into absolute, binding, and indissoluble communion with the world at large.' In a revealing phrase he says that individuation leads to 'a better social performance' (Jung, 1928a, pp. 174, 178).

This in fact proves to be so. In the most ordinary matters of everyday living we find, as we become more familiar with the unconscious factors that make us irritated, or unconfident, or ashamed, that our life becomes easier. We are more comfortable with and in our selves. We do indeed put in 'a better social performance' – at a party, when shopping, held up in a traffic jam, or coping with a teenager we find difficult or a partner who annoys us. The aim of therapy may not be directly to facilitate better

99

relationships; but this is a benevolent, very important, and inevitable consequence. 'Better' in the sense of 'more real' is not always the same as 'better' in the sense of 'more comfortable', as the delicate balance of projections and defences has often to be renegotiated at considerable cost.

Part of the process of individuation is to recognize and live more fully by one's own individual morality, even if it runs counter to the collective. There is obviously much space here for anxiety, unorthodoxy, and criminality. 'On paper the moral code looks clear and neat enough; but the same document written on the "living tables of the heart" is often a sorry tatter' (Jung, 1944, pp. 30f.). To move from living by the comprehensive moral code written on paper by others to living by the same document written in the stresses and passions of our own lives is very complicated.

To have the freedom either to observe the collective moral code or not is an ambiguous gift from the gods. Was it wrong for Adam and Eve to eat the apple? Their action was disobedient to God and lost them Paradise – but it gave them the knowledge of good and evil, the power and responsibility of choice, it gave them work, change, and children. They moved from a state of uncon-sciousness to one of ego-consciousness: it is the ego that has to evaluate and choose between opposing moral paths. The unconscious psyche is amoral: feelings just are. It needs direction from the ego, in tune with the self if not with the collective moral code.

Jung thought that '[t]he superego is a necessary and unavoidable substitute for the experience of the self' (Jung, 1940–1941, p. 260) – that '[m]orality is not imposed from outside; we have it in ourselves from the start' (Jung, 1917, p. 27). He suggests that we have an archetypal predisposition to understand and to order our experience in terms of right and wrong. Like any other archetype, this will be filled out with our personal experience – which includes our experience of our culture, both secular and religious, both parental and peer, and our own understanding of particular moral dilemmas that we meet as we grow up. So everyone's sense of right and wrong will have something of the collective in it, and something of the particular and the individual.

Any change in lifestyle or relationship is fraught with more or less difficulty and our beliefs or behaviour may seem to others eccentric. However, since we have become 'discontinuous' with the collective, in our own individuating process, we have a duty to sustain society, which we also need, by contributing something back to the collective well-being.

Personal morality: Malcolm

Malcolm belonged to a strict Protestant evangelical church that expelled members who had sex outside marriage. Yet, he was compulsively promiscuous. His conscious wish for obedience to authority and for sexual continence was constantly negated by his unconscious wish to rebel against authority, enacted through his sexuality. His ego was overwhelmed by this aspect of his self. However, very soon after starting therapy, Malcolm started enacting his wish to be disobedient within the therapy: he was late for sessions, he tramped in dirt from the pavement, he was constantly pushing the boundaries by forgetting to bring his cheque, and he was openly contemptuous of his therapist's clothes. Because he and his therapist could talk about these things, Malcolm came to understand that he had a wish to rebel; and so, instead of it being an unconscious wish that demanded expression, it became a moral problem about which he could think and make a choice. He was able to disentangle his feelings about his therapist and the therapy, and his feelings about his church's authority, from his experience of his step-father denying him access to his mother by sending him to live permanently with an aunt and uncle when their first child was born. He could think about his wish to disobey his step-father, and win his mother for himself. This enabled him over time to choose not to be so promiscuous, and after some more months he decided to leave his church and eventually settled into a fairly stable relationship.

When he was no longer caught in obeying or rebelling against the moral code written on paper by his church or his therapist, he became able to relate more fully to another.

The development of trust

Acknowledging a conversation between the conscious and the unconscious psyche necessarily recognizes that both exist. Images-perceived-as-symbols can then bridge the gap between them. This is a safe experience only when a person can trust both the strength and capacity of their ego and the essential usefulness of their unconscious psyche. This trust is usually built up gradually in therapy through the repeated experience of the therapist taking seriously every tiny manifestation of the unconscious psyche and demonstrating, by thinking about it, that it is possible for the ego to find the unconscious psyche both useful and manageable.

Such trust develops in parallel with a growing trust in another person and is a necessary condition for being able to think symbolically (Plaut, 1966). This is because we have to be able to tolerate not knowing the other totally and predictably – whether the 'other' is our own unconscious psyche or another person, whether it is what will happen inside us in phantasy or outside us in external reality.

REFERENCES

Astor, J. (1995). *Michael Fordham: Innovations in Analytical Psychology*. London: Routledge.

Beebe, B., & Lachman, F. M. (2002). *Infant Research and Adult Treatment*. Hillsdale, NJ: The Analytic Press.

Benvenuto, B., & Kennedy, R. (1986). *The Works of Jacques Lacan: An Introduction*. London: Free Association Books.

The Bible. New Revised Standard Version, anglicized edition. Oxford: Oxford University Press, 1989.

Bion, W. R. (1957). Differentiation of the psychotic from the non-psychotic personalities. In: *Second Thoughts: Selected Papers on Psycho-Analysis* (pp.43–64). London: Heinemann, 1967.

Bion, W. R. (1958). On hallucination. In: *Second Thoughts: Selected Papers on Psycho-Analysis* (pp. 65–85). London: Heinemann, 1967.

Bion, W. R. (1959). Attacks on linking. In: *Second Thoughts: Selected Papers on Psycho-Analysis* (pp.93–109). London: Heinemann, 1967.

Bion, W.R. (1962). A theory of thinking. In: *Second Thoughts: Selected Papers on Psycho-Analysis* (pp.110–119). London: Heinemann, 1967.

Bion, W. R. (1970). *Attention and Interpretation*. London: Tavistock.

Black, D. (1993). What sort of thing is a religion? A view from object-relations theory. *International Journal of Psycho-Analysis*, *74*: 613–625.

Bomford, R. (1999). *The Symmetry of God*. London: Free Association Books.

Britton, R. (1998). *Belief and Imagination: Explorations in Psychoanalysis*. London: Routledge.

Chamberlain, D. B. (1987). The cognitive newborn: a scientific update. *British Journal of Psychotherapy*, 4(1): 30–71.

Clark, M. (2003). Women's lack: the image of woman as divine. In: T. Adams & A. Duncan (Eds.), *The Feminine Case: Jung, Aesthetics and Creative Process* (pp.185–203). London: Karnac.

Everest, P. (1999). The multiple self: working with dissociation and trauma. *Journal of Analytical Psychology*, 44: 443–463.

Fonagy, P., Gergely, G., Jurist, E.L., & Target, M. (2002). *Affect Regulation, Mentalization, and the Development of the Self*. New York: Other Press.

Fordham, M. (1947). Defences of the self. In: *Explorations into the Self* (pp.152–160). London: Academic Press, 1985.

Fordham, M. (1955). The origins of the ego in childhood. In: *New Developments in Analytical Psychology* (pp.104–130). London: Routledge & Kegan Paul, 1957.

Fordham, M. (1957). Some observations on the self and the ego in childhood. In: *New Developments in Analytical Psychology* (pp.131–154). London: Routledge & Kegan Paul.

Fordham, M. (1973). Maturation of ego and self in infancy. In: M. Fordham, R. Gordon, J. Hubback, K. Lambert, & M. Williams (Eds.), *Analytical Psychology: A Modern Science* (pp. 83–94). London: Academic Press, 1980.

Fordham, M. (1978). *Jungian Psychotherapy*. London: John Wiley & Sons.

Fordham, M. (1985). *Explorations into the Self*. London: Academic Press.

Fordham, M. (1993). On not knowing beforehand. *Journal of Analytical Psychology, 38*: 127–136.

Freud, S. (1900a). *The Interpretation of Dreams. S.E. 4, 5*: 339–627. London: Hogarth.

Freud, S. (1915e). The unconscious. *S.E. 14*: 161–215. London: Hogarth.

Freud, S. (1916–1917). *Introductory Lectures on Psycho-Analysis. S.E. 15*. London: Hogarth.

Freud, S. (1917e). Mourning and melancholia. *S.E. 14*: 239–260. London: Hogarth.

Freud, S. (1918b). From the history of an infantile neurosis. *S.E. 17*: 3–122. London: Hogarth.

Freud, S. (1930a). Civilization and its discontents. *S.E. 21*: 59–145. London: Hogarth.

Freud, S. (1937c). Analysis terminable and interminable. *S.E. 23*: 211–253. London: Hogarth.

Freud, S. (1939a). Moses and monotheism. *S.E. 23*: 3–137. London: Hogarth.

Gordon, R. (1985). Big self and little self: some reflections. *Journal of Analytical Psychology, 30*: 261–271.

Gregory, R. L. (1966). *Eye and Brain: the Psychology of Seeing* (3rd edn, rev., 1986). London: Weidenfeld and Nicolson.

Guggenbühl-Craig, A. (1971). *Power in the Helping Professions.* Dallas, TX: Spring Publications.

Harlow, P. (1996). Malign individuation. Paper read to the Society of Analytical Psychology (unpublished).

Hillman, J. (1976). *Revisioning Psychology.* New York: Harper & Row.

Hinshelwood, R. D. (1989). *A Dictionary of Kleinian Thought.* London: Free Association Books.

Hubback, J. (1996). The archetypal senex: an exploration of old age. *Journal of Analytical Psychology, 41*: 3–18.

Jung, C. G. (1904). The associations of normal subjects. *C.W. 2*: 3–196.

Jung, C. G. (1907). The psychology of dementia praecox. *C.W. 3*: 1–151. London: Routledge & Kegan Paul.

Jung, C. G. (1916). General aspects of dream psychology. *C.W. 8*: 237–280. London: Routledge & Kegan Paul.

Jung, C. G. (1917). On the psychology of the unconscious. *C.W. 7*: 3–119. London: Routledge & Kegan Paul.

Jung, C. G. (1921). *Psychological Types. C.W. 6.* London: Routledge & Kegan Paul.

Jung, C. G. (1925). Marriage as a psychological relationship. *C.W. 17*: 187–201. London: Routledge & Kegan Paul.

Jung, C. G. (1928a). The relations between the ego and the unconscious. *C.W. 7*: 123–241. London: Routledge & Kegan Paul.

Jung, C. G. (1928b). Child development and education. *C.W. 17*: 49–62. London: Routledge & Kegan Paul.

Jung, C. G. (1929a). The aims of psychotherapy. *C.W. 16*: 36–52. London: Routledge & Kegan Paul.

Jung, C. G. (1929b). Problems of modern psychotherapy. *C.W. 16*: 53–75. London: Routledge & Kegan Paul.

Jung, C. G. (1930). The stages of life. *C.W. 8*: 387–403. London: Routledge & Kegan Paul.

Jung, C. G. (1939). Conscious, unconscious, and individuation. *C.W. 9i*: 275–289. London: Routledge & Kegan Paul.

Jung, C. G. (1940–1941). Transformation symbolism in the Mass. *C.W. 11*: 201–296. London: Routledge & Kegan Paul.

Jung, C. G. (1941). The psychology of the child archetype. *C.W. 9i*: 151–181. London: Routledge & Kegan Paul.

Jung, C. G. (1942). A psychological approach to the dogma of the Trinity. *C.W. 11*: 107–200. London: Routledge & Kegan Paul.

Jung, C. G. (1943). The spirit Mercurius. *C.W. 13*: 191–250. London: Routledge & Kegan Paul.

Jung, C. G. (1944). *Psychology and Alchemy. C.W. 12.* London: Routledge & Kegan Paul.

Jung, C. G. (1946). The psychology of the transference. *C.W. 16*: 163–323. London: Routledge & Kegan Paul.

Jung, C. G. (1947). On the nature of the psyche. *C.W. 8*: 159–234. London: Routledge & Kegan Paul.

Jung, C. G. (1951). *Aion. C.W. 9ii.* London: Routledge & Kegan Paul.

Jung, C. G. (1952a). Answer to Job. *C.W. 11*: 355–470. London: Routledge & Kegan Paul.

Jung, C. G. (1952b). *Symbols of Transformation. C.W. 5.* London: Routledge & Kegan Paul.

Jung, C. G. (1955–1956). *Mysterium Coniunctionis. C.W. 14.* London: Routledge & Kegan Paul.

Jung, C. G. (1957). The transcendent function. *C.W. 8*: 67–91.

Jung, C. G. (1962). *Memories, Dreams, Reflections.* New York: Pantheon. [Reprinted London: Fontana Paperbacks, 1983.]

Kalsched, D. (1996). *The Inner World of Trauma.* London: Routledge.

Kalsched, D. (1998). Archetypal defenses in the clinical situation: a vignette. *Journal of Analytical Psychology, 43*: 3–17.

Klein, M. (1937). Love, guilt and reparation. In: *Love, Guilt and Reparation,* (pp. 306–343). London: Hogarth Press, 1975.

Klein, M. (1940). Mourning and its relation to manic-depressive states. In: *Love, Guilt and Reparation* (pp. 344–369). London: Hogarth Press, 1975.

Klein, M. (1952). The mutual influences in the development of ego and id. In: *Envy and Gratitude* (pp. 57–60). London: Hogarth Press, 1975.

Klein, M. (1955). On identification. In: *Envy and Gratitude* (pp. 141–175). London: Hogarth Press, 1975.

Klein, M. (1959). Our adult world and its roots in infancy. In: *Envy and Gratitude* (pp. 247–263). London: Hogarth Press, 1975.

Knox, J. (2003). *Archetype, Attachment, Analysis.* Hove: Brunner-Routledge.

Kohut, H. (1984). *How Does Analysis Cure?* Chicago, ILL: University of Chicago Press.

Mahler, M., Pine F., & Bergman, A. (1975). *The Psychological Birth of the Human Infant.* London: Hutchinson.

Milrod, M. D. (2002). The concept of the self and the self representation. *Journal of Neuropsychoanalysis, 4*(1): 7–23.

Neumann, E. (1973). *The Child.* London: Hodder & Stoughton.

Pally, R. (2000). *The Mind–Brain Relationship.* London: Karnac.

Piontelli, A. (1992). *From Fetus to Child.* London: Routledge.

Plaut, A. (1966). Reflections on not being able to imagine. In: M. Fordham, R. Gordon, J. Hubback, K. Lambert, & M. Williams (Eds.), *Analytical Psychology: a Modern Science* (pp. 127–149). London: Academic Press, 1980.

Redfearn, J. W. T. (1985). *My Self, My Many Selves.* London: Academic Press.

Redfearn, J. W. T. (1992). *The Exploding Self.* Wilmette, IL: Chiron.

Robinson, H., & Fuller, V. G. (2003). *Understanding Narcissism in Clinical Practice.* London: Karnac.

Rosenfeld, H. A. (1987). *Impasse and Interpretation.* London: Tavistock.

Rycroft, C. (1968). *A Critical Dictionary of Psychoanalysis.* London: Nelson.

Samuels, A., Shorter, B., & Plaut, F. (1986). *A Critical Dictionary of Jungian Analysis.*London: Routledge & Kegan Paul.

Siegel, A. M. (1996). *Heinz Kohut and the Psychology of the Self.* London: Routledge.

Steiner, J. (1993). *Psychic Retreats.* London: Routledge.

Stern, D. N. (1985). *The Interpersonal World of the Infant.* New York: Basic Books.

Tennyson, A. (1842). The lotos-eaters. In: F. L. Lucas (Ed.), *Tennyson: Poetry and Prose* (pp. 45–50). Oxford: Clarendon Press, 1947.

Tresan, D. (1996). Jungian metapsychology and neurobiological theory. *Journal of Analytical Psychology, 41*: 399–436.

Urban, E. (1998). States of identity: a perspective drawing upon Fordham's model of the self. *Journal of Analytical Psychology, 43*: 261–276.

von Franz, M.-L. (1970). *Interpretation of Fairytales.* New York: Spring Publications.

Winnicott, D. W. (1945). Primitive emotional development. In: *Through Paediatrics to Psycho-Analysis* (pp. 145–156). London: Hogarth, 1958.

Winnicott, D. W. (1950). Aggression in relation to emotional development. In: *Through Paediatrics to Psycho-Analysis* (pp. 204–218). London: Hogarth, 1958.

Winnicott, D. W. (1951). Transitional objects and transitional phenomena. In: *Playing and Reality* (pp. 1–30). London: Tavistock, 1971 [reprinted London: Pelican Books, 1974].

Winnicott, D. W. (1960a). Ego distortion in terms of true and false self. In: *The Maturational Processes and the Facilitating Environment* (pp. 140–152). London: Hogarth Press, 1965.

Winnicott, D.W. (1960b). The theory of the parent-infant relationship. In: *The Maturational Processes and the Facilitating Environment,* (pp.37–55). London: Hogarth, 1965.

Winnicott, D. W. (1962). Ego integration in child development. In: *The Maturational Processes and the Facilitating Environment* (pp. 56–63). London: Hogarth, 1965.

Winnicott, D. W. (1963). From dependence towards independence in the development of the individual. In: *The Maturational Processes and the Facilitating Environment* (pp. 83–92). London: Hogarth, 1965.

Winnicott, D.W. (1969). The use of an object and relating through identifications. In: *Playing and Reality* (pp. 101–111). London: Tavistock, 1971 [reprinted London: Pelican Books, 1974].

Zinkin, L. (1991). The Klein connection in the London school: the search for origins. *Journal of Analytical Psychology, 36*: 37–62.

INDEX